Indiana's
1782 – 1791

History of the Northwest Territory - Part 1

Indiana History Time Line Series – Book 2

Paul R. Wonning

Indiana's Timeless Tales - 1782 – 1791
Published By Paul R. Wonning
Copyright 2017 by Paul R. Wonning
Print Edition

mossyfeetbooks@gmail.com

If you would like email notification of when new Mossy Feet books become available email the author for inclusion in the subscription list.

Mossy Feet Books
www.mossyfeetbooks.com

Indiana Places

http://indianaplaces.blogspot.com/

Description

Explore Indiana's early history using this journal of history stories from the beginning days of the Northwest Territory. *Indiana's Timeless Tales - 1782 – 1791* is a time line of events that shaped Indiana today. Many of the stories are little known and obscure historical tales.

Table of Contents

Indiana's Timeless Tales - 1782 – 1791

Paul R. Wonning

January, 08 1782 - John Vawter Born

John Vawter (January 8, 1782 - August 17 1862)

The son of Jesse and Elizabeth Watts Vawter, John was native to Orange County, Virginia. John gained his Baptist preacher license in 1804 and married Polly Smith on December 17, 1805. The couple had three children.

Move to Indiana

John and his father, along with several men from Scott and Franklin Counties in Kentucky traveled to Indiana sometime before 1806 on an exploratory mission. The men traveled in two parties, one party by land and another by water. The land party crossed the river at Port Milton. The other party traveled by canoe and landed at a point opposite Milton, Kentucky. The men explored and then returned to Kentucky. John came back to Indiana in May 1806, once again landing opposite Milton, Kentucky. After exploring the area again, he returned to Kentucky. He came back again in September with his brother in law, John Benhamr. John brought his family to settle in the Madison area in March 1807. John became the first magistrate of Madison and later served as the sheriff of Jefferson and Clark Counties. In 1810, he received appointment as U. S. Marshall in the Indiana Territory. He stayed in the Madison area until 1812, when he migrated into the area that would become Vernon. The beauty of the Muscatatuck area compelled him to stay. At this time Indians still inhabited the region and there was only one other white family in the area that would become Jennings County. During the War of 1812, Vawter served as part of the Indian Rangers and gained election as a colonel in the Jennings County militia in 1817. Vawter also worked as a surveyor and would take long surveying trips during this time.

Platting Vernon

Vawter platted Vernon, Indiana in 1815. By 1816, the new town had three cabins and the town soon grew. Vawter built the first schoolhouse in Jennings County and he organized the first Baptist Church in 1816. He gave every third lot to the new town. Polly Smith Vawter died in 1825 and John married her sister, Jane. Jane passed away in 1826. There were no children born to John and Jane, however Ruth Minton later. They would have three children. Ruth died in 1850 and John married Martha Pearce, with whom he had one daughter. A falling stack of lumber killed Martha in 1892.

Vawter served in the Indiana House of Representatives from 1831 until 1835 and in the Indiana Senate in 1836. He played a role in getting the 1836 Mammoth Internal Improvements Act passed while in the Senate. Vawter moved to Morgan County in 1848 and founded Morgantown.

February 17, 1782 - Colonel Robert Morgan Evans Born

Hugh McGary Jr. purchased 440 acres of land for a settlement on March 27, 1812. He named the new town McGary's Landing. He changed the name in 1814 to attract more settlement. The new name, Evansville, he chose in honor of Colonel Robert Morgan Evans.

Colonel Robert Morgan Evans (February 17, 1782 – December 14 1842)

The son of James Evans, Sr. and Elizabeth McMillan Evans, Robert was a native of Frederick County, Virginia. After migrating to Paris, Kentucky, he married Jane Trimble in 1803. A year later, the couple moved to Princeton, in the Indiana Territory. Four years later Evans moved to

Vincennes to open a tavern. During the War of 1812, he joined the militia at the rank of Captain. After the war, he received a promotion to brigadier general and returned to his original home in the Indiana wilderness. The voters elected him as the county clerk of Knox County, then to the Territorial Legislature. Around 1820 he moved to the McGary's settlement, which McGary had named after him. When the Harmonists began their experiment at New Harmony, he moved to join that community. When that experiment ended, he moved back to Evansville. The voters elected him to the Indiana House of Representatives. While in the legislature, he served as the Speaker of the House.

September 10, 1782 - John Ketcham Born

John Ketcham (1782-1865)

Keziah Pigmon Lewis Ketchem presented her husband, Daniel Ketcham, with their son on September 10, 1782 in Washington County, Maryland. The family migrated to Shelby County, Kentucky in 1784, where his Daniel built a fort, which the locals called Ketcham's Station. John married Elizabeth Pearey in 1802, with whom he had twelve children.

Move to Jackson County, Indiana

The couple migrated to Jackson County, Indiana in 1811. Native attacks had become a threat in the area, so Ketchem joined the Indiana Rangers and constructed a fort on his land, which was between Fort Vallonia and Huff's Fort. These outposts gave protection to the settlers during attacks, which were common during this time. The settlers generally worked their land during the daylight hours and slept nights within the confines of the forts. During the years, 1812 and 1813 Ketchem spent long periods on patrol and away from his family. During these campaigns, he gained the reputation as a fierce fighter. Gov. William Henry Harrison commissioned him as colonel in a regiment of the state's militia.

Monroe County

John moved to Harrodsburg, Indiana in 1818, where he built a gristmill on Clear Creek. Before leaving Jackson County, he sold the county 153 acres of land and donated a block to the county to use as the courthouse. During his time in Monroe County, he helped design the first courthouse and gained election to the Indiana Legislature. He also served as the first trustee for Indiana Seminary, which later became Indiana University. He also participated in the election of Andrew Jackson as elector in 1836. His remains lie in the Ketcham Family Cemetery, still maintained by Ketchem family members.

November 12, 1782 - William Hendricks Born

William Hendricks (November 12, 1782 – May 16, 1850)

The son of Abraham and Ann Jamison Hendricks, William was native to Ligonier Valley, Westmoreland County, Pennsylvania. He attended common school with future Indiana governor Jonathan Jennings. He enrolled in Jefferson College, where he studied until 1810, then moved to Ohio. He read law at Cincinnati and gained admittance to the bar. He then moved to Madison, in the Indiana Territory in 1813, a town he made his home the remainder of his life.

The Printer, the Politician

Hendricks bought a printing press and set up the second newspaper in Madison, The Western Eagle. He and Ann Parker Paul, the daughter of the founder of Madison, married. The couple would have two sons together, both of whom died in the Civil War. He gained election to the

Territorial Assembly, sat on the 1816 Constitutional Convention in Corydon and became the third governor of Indiana in 1822. He would also serve in the United States House of Representative and the Senate. Hendricks took sick while he supervised the construction of the family vault. He passed away later the same day, May 16, 1850.

Events of 1783

February 01, 1783 - Site for Clark's Grant Indiana Selected

The Virginia House of Burgesses had granted Clark and his men 150,000 acres of land in what is now southern Indiana as payment for his services during the Revolutionary War on January 2, 1781. The Assembly appointed ten commissioners, one of whom was George Rogers Clark, to apportion the land out to Clark and his men and to plat a town in the tract. The commissioners met on February 1, 1783 at Louisville to choose the site, which began at a spot south of the Falls of the Ohio and ran upriver to a point that would make the width of the tract equal to its length. The committee allotted 500 acres for a town they named Clarksville.

April 08, 1783 - Jacob Whetzel Born - Whetzel Trace

A man named Jacob Whetzel cut a road through the forest, beginning in 1818. Starting at Toner's Tavern in current Laurel, Indiana, the road cut into the lands of the New Purchase in central Indiana

Jacob Whetzel (Sep. 16, 1765 - Jul. 2, 1827)

Born near Big Wheeling Creek in West Virginia, Whetzler served in the Indian wars in West Virginia and Ohio, fighting under Generals William Henry Harrison and Arthur St. Clair. After the wars, he, his son Cyrus and four other men he hired cut a trail through the forests. His grave is in MacKenzie Cemetery, in Morgan County.

Edward Toner (April 8, 1783 - February 18, 1867)

Born in Lycoming Co., Pennsylvania to a father who came from Somerset, Ireland during the Revolutionary years, Edward moved to Franklin County, Indiana. Toner and his wife settled in a town named Somerset, a town he founded and named for his father's Irish home. He established the tavern that served as the trailhead for Whetzler's Trace.

"New Purchase"

The lands acquired from the Miami tribe by the terms of the Treaty with the Miami, 1818 (Treaty of St. Mary's), are referred to as the "New Purchase." Jonathan Jennings, Lewis Cass, and Benjamin Parke acting as representatives of the United States signed a treaty with the Miami nation on October 6, 1818. As per terms of the treaty, the Miami has ceded a vast area in central Indiana to the United States. The United States agreed to pay the Miami tribe fifteen thousand dollars a year, erect a gristmill and one sawmill. They would also provide a blacksmith and pay one hundred sixty bushels of salt a year to the tribe. After the agreement was reached, Whetzler cut the trace into the new lands and founded a small settlement of his own.

Excerpted from the author's book

Exploring Indiana's Historic Sites, Markers & Museums– Southeast Edition

http://mossyfeetbooks.blogspot.com/2015/11/blog-post.html

July 02, 1783 - Virginia Relieves George Rogers Clark of his Command

Virginia Governor Patrick Henry had authorized George Rogers Clark's campaign into the Illinois Country, later called the Northwest Territory. Clark had acted under the authority of Virginia and had never been part of the Continental Army. During the war, Clark had served under six Virginia governors. Governor Benjamin Harrison, the father of future Northwest Territory Governor William Henry Harrison, relieved George Rogers Clark of his command on July 2, 1783. The war effort had exhausted the financial resources of Virginia, so as hostilities wound down during the later stages of the Revolutionary War, Virginia had few resources.

Financial Straits

Clark had commanded the force that took the Illinois country from the British and as the commander, he had signed the requisitions for supplies that the force needed to operate during the campaign. On January 2, 1781, Virginia had granted Clark's men 150,000 acres on the north side of the Ohio River that included Clark's fort at the Falls of the Ohio. This land would form the foundation for the first settlements into what is now the State of Indiana. The Virginia legislature sent him a letter expressing sincere gratitude for his services; however, the financially exhausted Virginia did not offer to pay the expenses for the expedition that Clark had incurred. Thus, as his service to Virginia ended, the thirty-year-old George Rogers Clark found himself without employment and with no money. The government would not offer him a pension until five years before his death. It would take thirty years, after he had died, for the government to award him thirty thousand dollars for his services. The land-rich cash-poor Clark, whose share of the 150,000-acre grant was 8049 acres, would live in the area for most of the remainder of his life.

September 03, 1783 - Treaty of Paris signed - American War of Independence Over

Tireless and crafty American negotiators John Adams, Benjamin Franklin, and John Jay concluded discussions and signed the treaty that officially ended the American Revolution on September 3, 1783.

The key parts of the treaty included:

Great Britain recognized that the thirteen colonies were free and independent

Established the new nation's boundaries - including the lands of the Illinois Country north of the Ohio River

Granted fishing rights to United States fishermen in the Grand Banks, off the coast of Newfoundland and in the Gulf of Saint Lawrence

Recognition of debts to creditors by all parties

The United States Congress would attempt to get state legislatures to compensate British loyalists for land and property confiscated during the war

Prevent future confiscations of Loyalist wealth

Return all prisoners of war

Britain and United States receive perpetual access to the Mississippi River

Treaty must be ratified within sixty days of signing

Events of 1784

March 1, 1784 - Virginia Cedes Claim to Virginia Territory to United States

After a legal tug of war and many compromises, Virginia ceded the lands that became the Northwest Territory to the United States. The struggle had imperiled the ratification of the Articles of Confederation and threatened to turn the newly independent colonies into a struggle for land and power. Because of the cession, Maryland became the thirteenth state to ratify the Confederation and set the stage for Congress to form the Northwest Territory and eventual admittance of Ohio, Indiana, Illinois, Michigan, Wisconsin and Minnesota as states on equal footing with the original thirteen states.

Maryland Stalls Ratification

During the Revolutionary War, the Federal Government ran up debts of almost eight million dollars, a staggering sum for that day. The various States also had debts due to the war. Many of the States held claims to the lands west of the Appalachian Mountains. New York and Virginia had the largest claims. However, Massachusetts, Connecticut, North Carolina, South Carolina, Georgia also had extensive holdings. These claims totaled more than 222 million acres, a huge expanse.

Virginia's Huge Advantage

Maryland's chief complaint was that these states held a huge advantage over the landless states. This was because they could sell these lands to pay their debts. Marylanders felt that landless states like Maryland would have to levy heavy taxes to pay theirs off, stifling their growth.

Maryland feared that land rich states could operate with out any taxes, relying on the sale of these western lands for revenue. Maryland's residents would flee to the tax-free states. The impasse lasted almost four years.

Royal Charters

Virginia's claims originated in the second Royal Charter, granted by King James I. In it, he granted Virginia the lands of Maine south to the current North Carolina/South Carolina border. The lands were to extend "from sea to sea, west and northwest." this grant extended all the way to the Pacific Ocean, a staggering expanse of land. Revisions to this grant occurred over the years, but by the time of the Revolution, they still included lands claimed by Pennsylvania, New York and other colonies. When Virginian George Rogers Clark conquered Vincennes, Kaskaskia, Cahokia and other western outposts, he strengthened Virginia's claims to these regions. The Treaty of Paris had cut off the boundaries of the new nation at the Mississippi River. This still left Virginia and the other states with a vast territory to squabble over.

The Compromise

Congress and the states worked tirelessly to resolve the problems. New York, in a show of good faith, abandoned its land claims on January 17, 1780. Virginia followed suit on January 2, 1781, but they laid down conditions under which they would make it official. They wanted the Continental Congress to reimburse Virginia for the cost of George Rogers Clark's expedition, affirm all boundaries, affirm Virginia land claims in the disputed territories and reject all private claims in the cession area. This satisfied Maryland, which ratified the Articles on January 30, 1781. Congress did not accept the conditions, because many of the states still maintained their claims west of the Mississippi River. It took more negotiations to work out the problems and once again, Virginia renewed its offer on October 20, 1783, accepting Congress' recommendations. Congress accepted Virginia's cession on March 1, 1784. They had set the stage for the formation of the Northwest Territory and westward expansion.

March 27, 1784 - Jonathan Jennings Born

Jonathan Jennings, Indiana's First Governor was born on March 27, 1784.

Jonathan Jennings (March 27, 1784 – July 26, 1834)

Jonathan Jennings became the sixth child of Jacob and Mary Kennedy Jennings when he was born in New Jersey. He attended grammar school at Canonsburg, Pennsylvania, and studied law at Washington, Pennsylvania. He immigrated to the Indiana Territory in 1806 and became a lawyer in Jeffersonville, later moving to Vincennes. There were not enough clients in the new territory to make a living, so he served in various government offices and participated in several land speculation deals. These deals brought him some wealth. He and Territorial Governor Benjamin Harrison had a series of political disputes after Jennings became a clerk at Vincennes University.

Election to Congress

As a territory, the Indiana Territory was entitled to non-voting representation in Congress. Jennings gained election to the Eleventh Congress in 1809. In 1815, Jennings introduced a petition for Statehood to Congress. The 1815 census indicated that the population exceeded the 63000 requirement laid down by the Northwest Ordinance of 1787. Congress passed the Enabling Act on April 11, 1816, authorizing Indiana's authority to form a government. .

Constitutional Convention

He became a delegate to the Constitutional Convention in Corydon in June 1816. Jennings led the movement to ban slavery in the state. In this endeavor, he succeeded. The convention adjourned on June 29 and Jennings announced his candidacy for governor. He used the slogan "No Slavery in Indiana" during his campaign.

Governor Jennings

Jennings beat the other candidate, the former pro slavery Territorial Governor Thomas Posey handily. He served as governor for two terms, and returned to Congress as Indiana's elected representative in 1822. Jennings retired to his Charlestown home in 1831 after leaving Congress. He died at his Charlestown farm of a heart attack.

April 23, 1784 - Land Ordinance of 1784

The Land Ordinance of 1784 created an orderly procedure for the United States to deal with the lands west of the Allegheny Mountains that opened up by the compromises of 1781, 1782 and 1783 that led to the ratification of the Articles of   Confederation   in   1784.
Land Ordinance of 1784

Thomas Jefferson wrote the draft for the Land Ordinance of 1784. His draft included several important points:

The new states shall remain forever a part of the United States of America.

They shall bear the same relation to the confederation as the original states.

They shall pay their apportionment of the federal debts.

They shall in their governments uphold republican forms.

After the year 1800 there shall be neither slavery nor involuntary servitude in any of them

The proposed names of these states were Cherronesus, Assenisippia, Metropotamia, Sylvania, and Pelisipia

Passage

Congress considered Jefferson's draft and adopted it on April 23, 1784 after striking the slavery prohibition and the proposed names for the new states. This ordinance prepared the way for the Ordinance of 1785 that would provide a system for surveying the lands.

June 03, 1784 - First American Regiment Established

General George Washington had bid farewell to his officers after the Confederation Congress disbanded the Continental Army on December 4, 1783. The Congress created the First American Regiment on June 3, 1784, in large part to comply with requirements of the Treaty of Paris.

Requirements of the Treaty

The Treaty required the United States to occupy the British forts in the vast area that became the Northwest Territory. The treaty also charged the new nation with controlling white immigration into native territory. Their mission also included controlling conflicts that arose from settlers that intruded on native lands. Thus, Congress created the First American Regiment to accomplish those tasks. The First American Regiment was to build and garrison forts, help negotiate treaties with the Indians and help protect surveyors as they worked along the frontier.

First American Regiment

Also known as the Old Guard, the first recruits of the First American Regiment consisted primarily of units of the old Continental Army that Congress managed to persuade to enlist in the new force after mustering out of the Continental Army. The pay was bad, at only $6.67 per month. Congress had set a goal of 700 soldiers and officers for this regiment; however, the force probably never exceeded 450 men and about a dozen officers during the first few years of its existence. Congress authorized the force to consist of eight companies of infantry and two of artillery. The soldiers were mainly from four states, Pennsylvania, New Jersey, New York and Connecticut. The soldiers held commissions from their respective states, as the Congress had no law that authorized them to establish a military. Though the Regiment had plenty of weaponry, mostly leftover Continental Army muskets, the Congress did not have the means to feed or clothe this force properly.

Inefficient Command Structure

The Congress exercised direct control of the Regiment, utilizing a newly created Secretary at War to administer its commands. Under the Articles of Confederation that existed until 1787, the Congress was politically too weak to manage the regiment or protracted conflicts well.

Changes in Name

The regiment took up its first posting at Fort McIntosh in western Pennsylvania. Over the years, the regiment underwent many name changes and reorganizations. On September 29, 1789, it became the Regiment of Infantry. On March 3, 1791, it became the 1st Infantry. When Congress created the Legion of the United States, it was renamed the Infantry of the 1st Sub-Legion. The name 1st Infantry reemerged on October 31, 1796. In October 1815 the 1st, 5th, 17th, 19th, and the 28th Infantry regiments consolidated into a new force called the 3rd US Infantry Regiment, known as the Old Guard. This regiment still exists most consider it the oldest active military unit in the United States Army. The regiment mostly conducts memorial services for fallen soldiers. Primarily an infantry unit, the soldiers receive training in support roles for both domestic and overseas operations.

August 07, 1784 - Board of Trustees of the Town of Clarksville Meet at Louisville

The second meeting of the Board of Trustees met in Louisville to apportion some of the lands, settle some claims by Clark, his officers and soldiers. The Board also laid plans for completing the survey of the new town. The Board members kept no records of the first meeting.

August 12, 1784 - Josiah Harmar Appointed Commander of the First American Regiment

Congress appointed Josiah Harmar as "lieutenant colonel commandant" of the First American Regiment on August 12, 1784.

Josiah Harmar (November 10, 1753 – August 20, 1813)

The son of William Harmer and Rachel Harmer, Josiah was native to Philadelphia, Pennsylvania. He received his education at the Robert Proud's Quaker school.

American Revolution

At the beginning of the American Revolution, he enlisted in the 1st Pennsylvania Battalion in November 1775. A year later, he joined the 3rd Pennsylvania Regiment, commissioned as a captain. Harmar's military career showed a steady rise in command as he served in various Pennsylvania regiments in the Continental Army. His first action was at the Battle of Quebec on December 31, 1775. He later served with General George Washington at Valley Forge during the winter of 1777-78. During these years, he became acquainted with General George Washington, who considered him one of the best officers in the Army. Harmar would later serve with General Nathaniel Greene as his adjutant. By the end of the war, he had risen to the rank of lieutenant colonel.

Courier of Treaty of Paris

After Congress ratified the Treaty of Paris at the end of the Revolutionary War, Congress appointed Harmar as the courier to convey the ratified treaty to Benjamin Franklin in Paris. In 1784, Harmar married Sarah Jenkins, with whom he would have four children.

October 22, 1784 - Treaty of Fort Stanwix (1784)

During the negotiations for the Treaty of Paris in 1783, neither the Americans nor the British took the state of the Indian nations in the former colonies into consideration. The British, who had always taken care of the natives, virtually abandoned them when they withdrew all their military forces after the treaty's signing.

Uncertain Relations

The relationship between the natives and the new American government was one of uncertainty and suspicion. Native attacks on whites living on the frontier still occurred, with many settlers dying or taken prisoner in the attacks. The new United States government could not decide at first who was responsible for negotiating with the Indian nations, the Federal Government or the states. At the end of the Revolutionary War, several Indian tribes still inhabited Western Pennsylvania. President George Washington and most Pennsylvanians wanted to drive them out and establish the boundaries of the nation. Pennsylvania officials at first tried to deal with the problem, but Congress decided that it was the Federal Government's responsibility to negotiate with the tribes. The treaty negotiations would take place at Fort Stanwix in western New York, near present day Rome.

Treaty of Fort Stanwix

The Treaty of Fort Stanwix was the first treaty between the Indian nations and the United States. The goal of the United States government was to drive the natives from Pennsylvania, ending the attacks and freeing the prisoners. The meetings included representatives of the League of The Iroquois, which included the Mohawks, Oneidas, Onodagas, Cayugas, and Senecas. The treaty, upon its signing, recognized each tribe as a sovereign nation and established an Indian reserve called the Cornplanter Reserve in Pennsylvania. The Iroquois agreed to move out of western Pennsylvania and ceded lands in the Great Lakes region, which would include the future states of Indiana, Kentucky and Ohio. The tribe had laid claim to this vast area after dominating it during the Beaver Wars in the Seventeenth Century.

After the Treaty

Pennsylvania concluded a land deal with the tribe soon after the treaty's signing and the Iroquois moved out of the state. However, the League of The Iroquois did not ratify the agreement and the Indian tribes to the west of Pennsylvania refused to honor it, as they contended that the Iroquois did not live in the Ohio River Valley or Great Lakes region and had no right to cede it.

Events of 1785

January 21, 1785 - George Rogers Clark Helps Negotiate the Treaty of Fort McIntosh

Hoping to quell problems with the native tribes, the Congress sent George Rogers Clark, Arthur Lee, and Richard Butler to Fort Mackintosh to negotiate a treaty with the tribes that had not attended negotiations at Fort Stanwix.

Fort Mackintosh

Located on the extreme western border of Pennsylvania, Fort Mackintosh guarded the mouth of the Beaver River where it drained into the Ohio River. Built in 1778, the fort derives its name from General Lachlan McIntosh, commander Western Department of the Continental Army, which had its headquarters at Fort Pitt. The First American Regiment, organized in 1784, garrisoned Fort Mackintosh until the fort's closure in 1791. The trapezoid-shaped fort had 150-foot long sides and raised earth bastions on each corner. A deep ditch provided protection on three sides and the Ohio River protected the fourth. The fort had three barracks for the soldiers and officers quarters. The fort also had a blacksmith shop, kitchen and munitions magazines.

Treaty Negotiations

Representatives of the Delaware, Wyandot, Chippewa, and Ottawa tribes attended the meetings at the fort, which began in early January. There was actually very little negotiation. The United States representatives reminded the natives that they had sided with the British in the conflict and that the Americans, under George Rogers Clark, had conquered the region. The natives that attended were mostly young chiefs with little or no authority to negotiate a treaty. The Americans plied them with alcohol, and they signed the treaty on January 21, 1785.

The Terms

The tribes agreed that they lived under the protection of the American government and it forbade them from forming alliances with foreign powers. The tribes ceded most of what would become eastern and southern Ohio, northeastern Indiana and portions of Michigan. The United States promised to prevent squatters from settling in the lands reserved for the natives. The treaty deprived the Shawnee, who had not attended, of their valuable southwest Ohio lands. None of the tribal leaders accepted the treaty, which did not bring the peace that the Americans hoped it would.

May 20, 1785 - Land Ordinance of 1785

The Land Ordinance of 1785 set the stage for the orderly development of the western lands designated as the Northwest Territory by the Ordinance of 1784. This Ordinance had laid the lay the groundwork for development of the vast region that would become Ohio, Indiana, Illinois, Michigan and Wisconsin. The Ordinance of 1784 did not create a system for dividing, surveying and selling these lands. The Land Ordinance of 1785 created this system and more. It also established a method of lands for public education and government in the new lands.

The Treaty of Paris - 1783

The Treaty of Paris officially ended the Revolutionary War. Under the terms of the treaty, the new United States acquired the vast territory west of the Appalachian Mountains between the Great Lakes, the Mississippi River and the Ohio River. Congress had various problems in dealing with this vast area. The first was to deal with the states that claimed this area. It had to solve this problem before the last state to ratify the Articles of Confederation, Maryland, would ratify. Virginia resolved this problem on

March 1, 1784 when it ceded its claims to the Confederation Congress. Maryland ratified a short time later, and the Confederation came to life.

Native Tribes Did Not Recognize United States Claims

Another huge problem was that the Amerindian tribes in the region did not wish to recognize the new United States as the new administrator of the area. Congress would resolve this issue through a series of treaties that ceded the land, bit by bit, to the new nation. This was important to the Congress, because the Articles of Confederation did not allow the Congress to levy taxes on its citizens. The creation of a system of land acquisition and sales would provide a revenue stream for the United States. The Land Ordinance of 1785 set up this system of land acquisition and survey. The Congress needed this system. To do this, the delegates appointed a committee.

Committee Design the System

The Confederation Congress appointed five men to design this system. These men were:

Thomas Jefferson (Virginia)

Hugh Williamson (North Carolina)

David Howell (Rhode Island)

Elbridge Gerry (Massachusetts)

Jacob Read (South Carolina)

Designing the Survey System

After the Ordinance of 1784 passed Congress, these men worked to design a land survey system. There were two basic systems used during the colonial period the men used to design their system. These systems had worked well during colonial times and the designers used elements of both to design their plan. The New England system was the one they used as a basic guide. This system included land set aside for public education, government and churches, basic needs Congress felt necessary for a developing society. The Southern system encouraged people to claim land, have it surveyed and then live on it.

Problems

Two key problems were that this system allowed men to claim large areas of land, but not hold clear title to it. It also encouraged the formation of plantations that used slave labor. Many historians feel that Jefferson favored a system that did not allow for the formation of plantations. Smaller plots discouraged slave labor. Jefferson did not want slavery extending into the new territory.

System of Survey

The Ordinance called for dividing the territory into a basic land unit called a township. The township was to be six miles square, or thirty-six square miles. Surveyors would then divide each township into one-mile square units called sections. Each of these contained 640 acres. Each section was systematically numbered. Congress set a price of one dollar per acre, with a full section selling for $640.

Reserved Sections

The Ordinance reserved the central section, Section 16, aside for public education. It also designated Sections 8, 11, 26, and 29 for Congress to grant to Revolutionary War veterans as compensation for their war service. The Congress had no money to pay these men, so it could now award them grants of land. Congress also established land offices for people to buy the land.

Point of Beginning

All surveys need a point of beginning, and the Northwest Territory was no different. Surveyors established this Point of Beginning at the junction of Ohio Pennsylvania and

Virginia on the north shore of the Ohio River. This point is near East Liverpool, Ohio. An historical marker now marks the Point of Beginning.

August 15, - 1785 - John Clark Purchases Farm Near Louisville, Kentucky

George Rogers Clark had settled in the Louisville, a settlement that he had helped found during his Illinois campaign in 1779.

Convincing his Family to Move

He explored the area while writing letters to his parents that they should move from their Virginia home to Louisville. He settled a piece of property on what is now the east side of Louisville, near the south fork of Beargrass Creek and about three miles from the Ohio River. The Clark family did decide to relocate in 1784. They traveled to Redstone Landing, at the spot the Redstone Creek empties into the Monongahela River in southwestern Pennsylvania, where they spent the winter. They began their journeyed down the Monongahela and the Ohio embarking on their voyage down the Ohio River, arriving sometime in March 1785. Some historians think that George, his brother Jonathan and some family slaves built the cabin the Clarks would live in. The Clarks brought George's four younger siblings with them when the moved. These included Lucy, Elizabeth, William, and Frances.

Mulberry Hill

John Clark initially named the estate "Ampthill, to honor an estate in Virginia owned by friends and family of the Clark family. However, after a few years he renamed it Mulberry Hill. The cabin and outbuildings stood until around 1900, when it fell down as was demolished. At the beginning of World War I, the Federal government purchased the property, razed the few remaining buildings, and established Camp Zachary Taylor. After the war, the Clark family purchased about forty acres of the original estate where the original house had stood and donated it to the City of Louisville to use as a park.

George Rogers Clark Park

1024 Thruston Ave.

Louisville, KY 40217

https://louisvilleky.gov/government/parks/park-list/george-rogers-clark-park

Autumn 1785 - Construction of Fort Harmar Begins

The problems of white incursions into Amerindian territory threatened to create greater conflict between the Americans and the native tribes of the Ohio River Valley. Thus, the primary purpose of Fort Harmar when American troops constructed it was to keep whites from settling in the native lands north of the Ohio River.

Construction

Major John Doughty received orders from his superior officer, General Josiah Harmar, to build a new fort at the mouth of the Muskingum River in the current state of Ohio. Construction began in the fall and continued through spring. He located the fort on the west side of the Muskingum. Upon completion, Doughty named the new fort after his superior officer. The pentagon-shaped fort featured horizontal log walls with bastions to help support them. Four palisades offered an elevated field of vision for defenders. Two story buildings inside the fort provided quarters for officers and men. The arsenal was in a tower that doubled as a watchtower. After construction, Doughty had the troops plant a garden to supply food for the troops.

Evicting Settlers

Periodically, trained solders called rangers would issue forth from the fort, two or three at a time. Their primary purpose was to look for signs of whites that had settled north of the Ohio River, however they also watched for signs of native activity. If they found a settler in native lands, they had the authority to remove them. Fort Harmar remained active until 1790, when the Army transferred most of the remaining garrison to Fort Washington, at the mouth of the Miami River. The army deactivated the fort in 1795.

October 22, 1785 - Fort Finney Established

About a year after the Treaty of Fort Stanwix's signing, the United States government had arranged for treaty negotiations with the tribes that had not attended the previous treaty council. The government decided to build a fort to protect the negotiation team, so in early October the army dispatched a company of soldiers to build a fort. The company, led by Captain Walter Finney, arrived on the site on October 22, 1785 and immediately began constructing the fort.

Walter Finney (1747 - September 17, 1820)

The son of Walter and Jean Stephenson Finney, William was native to New London, Pennsylvania. Raised as a farmer, Finney enlisted in the Continental Army at the beginning of the Revolutionary War with the rank of Lieutenant. He served at the Battle of Brandywine on September 11, 1777 and received a wound to the head from a cannon firing grapeshot. The British captured him, imprisoning him on a prisoner of war ship anchored in New York harbor. He was part of a prisoner exchange, thus escaping the starvation imposed by their British captors. After he finished his military service, Finney returned to his farm in Pennsylvania, gaining election as a judge in 1790. He died on his farm on September 17, 1820 and is interred at Thunder Hill Cemetery in New London.

Fort Finney

Finney had his soldiers build the fort at the mouth of the Miami River at the site of the current Duke Energy power plant. The fort remained occupied for a short time after the treaty signing on January 31, 1786. The fort was abandoned, possibly replaced by the Fort Finney constructed at the Falls of the Ohio near present day Jeffersonville in 1786.

December 06, 1785 - John Van Cleve Family Arrives Washington, Pennsylvania

Blacksmith John Van Cleve, his wife Catherine and eight children arrive at Washington, Pennsylvania.

John Van Cleve (May 16, 1749 - June 1, 1791)

The son of Benjamin and Rachel Covenhoven Van Cleve, John was native to New Brunswick, Middlesex County, New Jersey Colony. At fifteen, John apprenticed to a blacksmith in Freehold, New Jersey. By 1771, John had finished his apprenticeship and established a blacksmith shop. That year he met, and married, Catherine Benham. The couple would have nine children, three of whom would die in infancy.

American Revolution

After the Battles of Lexington and Concord occurred, the New Jersey militia mobilized. John enlisted in the militia and served in his father's company. In that capacity, he acted as a guide for Captain Daniel Morgan's company of Riflemen. He continued to serve in the New Jersey militia after Morgan's capture at the Battle of Quebec on December 31, 1775. He served under General David Forman of the Continental Army during the American loss at the Battle of Germantown on October 4, 1777. After the battle, the British occupied Philadelphia. Van Cleve joined scouting parties that harassed British troops that had left the city to search for supplies.

Battle of Monmouth

By May of 1778, the British departed Philadelphia and began their march towards New York. General Washington pursued them, catching them at Monmouth, New Jersey, resulting in the Battle of Monmouth on June 28, 1778. Van Cleve's family fled in confusion to the Pine Swamps as the battle developed around them. John left them to help Morgan's company reorganize itself in the confusion of battle. Musket fire terrified the hiding family as the battle raged. The Americans prevailed, driving the British from the field, leaving devastation in their wake. The British had cut down the orchards, killed livestock and left the countryside in a state of charred destruction. John found his anvil in the ruins of his blacksmith shop and all that remained alive was a heifer and a sow that had its back broken by a British saber. This was the last battle of the Revolution that John served in during the Revolution.

Move to Washington, Pennsylvania

John's brother in law, Robert Benham, had settled in Washington, Pennsylvania, which is southwest of Pittsburg. He had traveled in early 1785 to Van Cleve's home in Freehold to visit John and convince him to near his home near the Monongahela River. John finally agreed to migrate, so the family, which had lived in the New Jersey area for over 100 years, decided to pull up stakes and move to the frontier area of southwestern Pennsylvania.

The Beginning

The family spent most of the summer preparing for the move. Finally, on November 2, 1785 the caravan of four wagons, eight horses and the entire Van Cleve family boarded their wagons and began the long journey to Washington, Pennsylvania. His thirteen-year-old son, Benjamin drove the lead wagon, with his mother beside him. Robert Benham drove another wagon and John's apprentice

Tunis Voorheis drove another. Two of the daughters, ages seven and ten, walked alongside the wagon while four-year-old William and one-year-old George rode in the wagon with their mother. John rode a horse and rode ahead to scout the path. The author does not know who drove the fourth wagon. Three wagons held the family's possessions, the fourth John's blacksmith supplies.

The Journey

The family covered thirty miles the first day, the most they would cover for the entire thirty-four day journey of almost 400 miles. The camped about sixteen miles from Philadelphia in country that had been almost denuded of forests after almost 100 years of settlement. The next day they managed to find the Pennsylvania Road, which was little more than a rutted path leading west into the densely forested hilly area of southern Pennsylvania. Travel was slow. The road had no bridges, so the family had to ford each river and stream. The road ascended the steep hills using hairpin curves to gain the summit. The hills were so steep, they had to unhitch two horses from one wagon and add it to the next so the horses could gain the summit. After reaching the summit, they tied ropes to the wagons and lowered them down using raw muscle until they got to into the valley. They would then start the process over again for the next wagon until all were down. Then they would ascend the next hill. As winter approached, the family endured snow and ice. Wagons broke down periodically, and they would lose a day repairing the wagon. At length, they reached their destination on December 6, 1785. They lived in the Washington Pennsylvania area until 1790, when they would once again migrate to Losantiville in the Northwest Territory.

December 16, 1785 - James Noble Born

James Noble (Dec. 16, 1785 - Feb. 26, 1831)

The son of Dr. Thomas Noble and Elizabeth Clair Sedgwick, James was native to Berryville, Virginia. The family moved to the frontier region of Campbell County, Kentucky around 1795. Around 1802 he married Mary Lindsay, with whom he would have six children. After his marriage, Noble studied law with a Mr. Southgate and attained his law license.

Move to the Indiana Territory

Upon attaining this, he migrated to Brookville, Indiana sometime around 1808. He opened a law office in Brookville and operated a ferryboat. By 1810, he received an appointment as prosecuting attorney for Franklin and Wayne Counties. Territorial Governor Thomas Posey appointed him as a circuit judge on April 25, 1815. He gained a favorable reputation with the voters in the Brookville area, who elected him to the Constitutional Convention in 1816. He next gained election to the first Indiana General Assembly in the August election. He took his seat on November 4, 1816.

First of Indiana's Senators

On November 8, 1816, the Indiana General Assembly elected him as one of Indiana's first two United States Senator, a post Noble held until his death.

Events of 1786

January 31, 1786 - Treaty of Fort Finney

The Shawnee tribe had not attended negotiations at the Treaty of Fort Stanwix or the Treaty of Fort McIntosh. Thus, they did not accede to its terms. War loomed and the United States sought to avoid it, so the government had arranged for treaty negotiations at the mouth of the Miami River and had built Fort Finney to protect their negotiators, who included George Rogers Clark, Richard Butler, and Samuel Parsons. Native tribes included the Shawnee and the Delaware.

The Negotiations

Over 300 warriors, painted for war and angry squeezed into the fort's council house. The negotiations did not go well. The United States demanded that the tribe give up its lands in what would become southwestern Ohio and southern Indiana. The Shawnee lived in the Ohio lands, used the Indiana hills as a hunting ground, and refused. Shawnee chiefs thrust a black wampum belt, a sign of war, at Clark, who tossed it aside. The Americans threatened to attack them if they did not accept the terms. Fearing American power, the tribe's negotiators finally gave in and signed the treaty.

The Treaty

The terms of the treaty demanded that the tribe give up any prisoners that they held, vacate the lands north of the Ohio River and acknowledged the sovereignty of the United States. The United States promised to keep squatters from settling in what remained of native lands. Later that year the Congress would pass the act that organized the Northwest Territory, setting the stage for the territory's settlement and further development into states. The natives, though they signed the treaty, did not give up their lands without a fight. The Northwest Indian Wars loomed in the future.

March 01, 1786 - Ohio Company of Associates Organized

A group of New England men that included Rufus Putnam, Benjamin Tupper, Samuel Holden Parsons and Manasseh Cutler met at the Bunch-of-Grapes Tavern in Boston, where they formed the Ohio Company of Associates.

Ohio Company of Associates

The men used the company to forge plans to settle areas along the north bank of the Ohio River in what was native land at the time. The Ohio Company first purchased 1,500,000 acres from the United States along the river at the mouth of the Muskingum. The group founded Marietta at this site about a year later. The Company acquired 750,000 additional acres land along the Scioto River later in 1786.

April 15, 1786 - Battle of the Embarrass River

In retaliation for an ambush sprung by a band of Piankeshaw warriors on a boat sailing on the Wabash River, a group of men from Vincennes, led by John Small, Moses Henry, and Daniel Sullivan attacked a Piankeshaw village that was located on the Wabash River near the mouth of the Embarrass River.

Piankeshaw

The Piankeshaw tribe was a tribe that spoke an Algonquin dialect and was part of the Miami tribe, though they maintained separate villages. Most of these villages were in the western portion of what is now Indiana and mostly scattered along the White River and the Vermillion River in Illinois. The Piankeshaw village near Vincennes was south of the town. The tribe had maintained mostly friendly relations with the Americans and had even provided aid to George Rogers Clark during his Illinois campaign. However, in the years after the Revolutionary War American squatters had begun settling in their lands. About seventy families of settlers had settled illegally on Piankeshaw land. Infuriated, the Piankeshaw began harassing settlers in and around Vincennes. After the attack on the boat, the Vincennes settlers had had enough and planned a retaliatory attack.

The Battle of the Embarrass River

The Americans attacked the village, however the attackers got the worst of the ensuing battle as the defending Piankeshaw warriors killed and wounded several of the attackers. There is no mention of Piankeshaw casualties. The Americans withdrew. Shortly after the battle, the Piankeshaw abandoned the village, with most moving north along the Wabash to the tribe's main village, at the mouth of the Vermillion River, which is north of present day Terre Haute. .

Daniel Sullivan (1754/5-1790)

At nine years of age, a band of Delaware warriors captured Daniel and his brother. Native families adopted the boys. Their village was on the Muskingum River in current southwestern Ohio. In 1772, the boys went in company with a native trading party to Fort Pitt, at the Forks of the Ohio. A brother in law recognized the boys and bought them from the natives. Sullivan served as a guide for the militia during Lord Dunmore's War in 1774. During the Revolutionary War he was arrested twice while serving as a scout and spy for the Americans. The British released him both times. In 1785, he departed the home he had established in Louisville for Vincennes to lead the Indiana militia. After leading the militia at the Battle of the Embarrass River in southeastern Illinois, native warriors killed him somewhere along the

Buffalo Trace in 1790 while carrying a message from Louisville to Vincennes.

Moses Henry (c.1746 - 1789)

The son of John Henry, Moses was probably native to Lancaster, Pennsylvania. Trained as a gunsmith, he worked at Fort Pitt in 1766 for the firm of Baynton, Wharton, and Morgan. He migrated first to an Indian village called Chillicothe to work as a gunsmith for the Shawnees around 1772. Sometime around 1779 he moved to Vincennes, where he died in 1789.

July 15, 1786 - Piankeshaw Warriors Return to Vincennes

On July 15, 1786 about 450 Piankeshaw warriors in forty-seven war canoes returned from their village on the Vermillion River intent upon massacring the population of Vincennes and destroying the town. John Philip Marie Legras and François Riday Busseron played a critical role in diffusing the situation, but not before the warriors had killed one resident and wounded a few others.

John Philip Marie Legras

The author has been unable to find much information about Colonel Legrass other than that Clark had promoted him to lieutenant colonel of the local militia in July 20, 1779 during his conquest of Vincennes. Legrass and Busseron had hidden gunpowder and lead bullets from the British by burying them when the British reoccupied Vincennes. He also appointed him as commandant of the village and president of the town's court. He was also one of the leaders of the flotilla that had captured British supplies on the March 2, 1779 "Westernmost Naval Battle of the American Revolution". Most considered him one of Vincennes leading citizens. He is buried in the Old French Cemetery.

François Riday Busseron (1748 - 1791)

Busseron operated a general store and worked as a fur trader at the time Clark captured Vincennes from the British. He served as captain of the local militia. When Father Gibault came to Vincennes with tidings of the French alliance with the United States, Busseron decided to take the side of the Americans. He and Legras provided valuable aid to Clark during his conquest by supplying them with gunpowder and ball when their own powder was ruined when they waded through the deeply flooded Wabash River. When Clark promoted Legrass to colonel, he promoted Busseron to major at the same time. He also accompanied Leonard Helm on his mission to capture British supplies in March 1779. Clark had left him in charge of Fort Patrick Henry in Vincennes when he departed in 1780. Busseron had advanced a great deal of money to Clark during the expedition, impoverishing himself and his family in the process. The Bosseron family never received compensation. Bosseron is buried in the Old French Cemetery.

July 22, 1786 - John Small Drafts Letter to George Rogers Clark Requesting Aid

The incident of July 22 had frightened the residents of Vincennes. Thus on July 22, 1786 John Small and Colonel John Philip Marie Legras sent a letter to George Rogers Clark requesting his aid in defending the village against further Indian attacks.

John Small (1759-1821)

A noted gunsmith, Small and his family immigrated to Pennsylvania while John was a child. He apprenticed as a gunsmith, a craft in which he excelled. During the Revolutionary War, he served in the militia at Fort Pitt. At war's end, John Small migrated to Vincennes. In addition to his gunsmith business, he also worked as a merchant, and tavern owner. He had taken part in the action at Embarrass River. Later on, he received appointment as Sheriff of Knox County on July 4, 1790. This gives him the distinction of being the first sheriff in the Indiana Territory. He would also gain election as a representative of Vincennes to the Northwest Territorial Assembly in 1800. Indiana Territorial Governor William Henry Harrison appointed him as the territory's first adjutant general. His tavern would be the site of Indiana Territorial Assembly in 1813 and as the first Knox County Courthouse.

August 14, 1786 - John Tipton Born

John Tipton (August 14, 1786 – April 5, 1839)

John was born in Sevier County, Tennessee, where his father died in an Amerindian raid. He moved to Harrison County, Indiana in 1803 and married Martha Shields. He farmed and fought natives, leading a unit of the famed Yellow Jackets during the Battle of Tippecanoe. His next military experience was commanding Fort Vallonia as major during the War of 1812. He gained election to the Indiana State House of Representatives from 1819 to 1823. During this time, he was involved in the formation of Bartholomew County and its county seat, Columbus.

September 09, 1786 - Clark Departs Clarksville with 1000 Men

Aware of the unrest, George Rogers Clark had been planning a campaign in the Vincennes area since the spring. When he received John Small's letter, he petitioned the local United State Army commander at Fort Finney, Lieutenant Colonel Josiah Harmar, to help the citizens of Vincennes.

Clark Sets Out On His Own

Harmar's orders from his superiors forbade him from launching an offensive war against the natives. Thus, Harmar denied Clark's request. Clark would not take no for an answer, so he recruited a force of over 1000 men and set out from Clarksville on the Vincennes Trace on September 9, 1786.

Reputation as a Leader Declined

Clark's expedition turned out to be a disaster. The force reached Vincennes; however, most of the men mutinied and deserted. In the spring of 1787, he launched an unauthorized campaign against Kaskaskia. His actions angered the United States Government, which reacted by sending Harmar to Vincennes to deal with Clark.

1786 – Beginnings of Jeffersonville Indiana

History

Fort Finney

Jeffersonville, Indiana has its roots in a fort constructed in 1786 across the river from Louisville, Kentucky. Captain Walter Finney established the fort, naming it Fort Finney. It was located at the site of the Kennedy Bridge. The fort's purpose was to protect the growing white population from depredations by the Indians, which still populated the area. The square earth and timber fort had blockhouses at the corners facing the river. Barracks for the soldiers formed a part of the wall. A protective trench extended from the river and surrounded the fort. The fort was renamed Fort Steuban in 1787 and abandoned by 1793.

Jeffersonville Established

Lieutenant Isaac Bowman, brother to Joseph Bowman, had received a portion of land as his share of Clark's Grant. He endeavored to have a town laid out on the 150-acre tract and commissioned George Rogers Clark's cousin, Marston Green Clark, in company with William Goodwin, Richard Pile, Davis Floyd and Samuel Gwathmey to plat the town and begin selling lots. The men platted the town on June 23, 1802 using a city design grid devised by Thomas Jefferson. They named the new town Jeffersonville, in honor of President Thomas Jefferson, who gained election to the presidency in 1800.

Isaac Bowman (April 24, 1757 – September 9, 1826)

The son of George Bowman and Mary Hite, Isaac was native to Frederick County, Virginia. His father died in 1768, when Isaac was eleven, and bequeathed him a part of the estate, Harmony Hall on Cedar Creek, near Strasburg. The brothers, in company with Isaac Hite, migrated into Kentucky in 1775, settling in the area of Warren County, Kentucky. He and his three brothers, Colonel John Bowman, Colonel Abraham Bowman, and Major Joseph Bowman all served during the Revolutionary War. Isaac and his brother Joseph joined the George Rogers Clark campaign. Isaac Bowman was part of the company that escorted Henry Hamilton and other British prisoners from Vincennes to Williamsburg, Virginia after Clark and his men captured Vincennes. He paid his brother Joseph's funeral expenses after he died of the severe burns suffered as part of the men celebrating their capture of the city. Bowman received a portion of Clark's Grant in payment for his war services. Bowman took part commanding a party of settlers that departed from Kaskaskia in November 1779. A band of Chickasaw warriors captured the settlers. Many considered Bowman dead, as no news came of him until he resurfaced in Shenandoah, Virginia in 1782. He had managed to escape the tribe and had made a harrowing return via Cuba. He settled on the family estate and married Elizabeth Gatewood, with whom he had four children. He married

Mary Chinn after Elizabeth died in 1800. He had nine more children with Mary.

Thomas Jefferson (April 13, 1743 – July 4, 1826)

The son of Peter Jefferson and Jane Randolph, Thomas was native to Shadwell, Virginia. A local minister with private tutors and later a private school taught his early education. Jefferson's education was extensive, including studies of Greek, French, natural history, mathematics, metaphysics, and philosophy. He enrolled at the College of William & Mary in Williamsburg, Virginia, at sixteen years old. He graduated two years later. Jefferson gained a law license and read many books from the English and ancient classics. His love of books led to a collection that would total over 6,500 volumes. His library would form the basis of the Library of Congress after the British burned it during the War of 1812.

Early Years

During these early years Jefferson developed many of the views that would shape his legacy and the nation he helped birth. His love of farming led to his belief that it the United States should base its economy on agriculture and not industry. As a lawyer, he worked at reforming slavery, taking several cases for slaves trying to gain emancipation. Upon losing one of the cases, Jefferson gave his client some money. The slave later escaped. This case was the first time he used Natural Law, the belief that all rights are inherent by virtue of human nature. He would develop this more fully later in the Declaration of Independence. By 1767, Jefferson was ready to begin the political career that would create a nation and change the world.

Fledgling Politician

His father died when Thomas was twenty years old, after which he inherited the 5000-acre plantation that included Monticello. Jefferson's political career began with his election to the Virginia House of Burgesses in 1767. He married Martha Wayles Skelton in 1772, with whom he would have six children. His public career as a founding father is without precedent. He authored the Declaration of Independence, served in Congress and was the main author of the Land Ordinance of 1784, which established the Northwest Territory. He was serving in France as Minister to France during the negotiations that formed the Constitution. After his return, he served President Washington as the first Secretary of State. He then gained election to the Presidency himself in 1800. As President, he would fight the United States first wars, the Barbary Wars, and engineered the Louisiana Purchase, which nearly doubled the land area of the fledgling United States. This acquisition spurred the famous Lewis and Clark Expedition that set out from the Falls of the Ohio. He retired from public life after his second term ran out. He would die on the fiftieth anniversary of the Declaration of Independence. By coincidence, another founding father, John Adams, died the same day. He was interred at Monticello. He still wore a locket containing a lock of his wife, Martha's hair. Martha had died in 1782.

Early History

The plat loosely followed Jeffersonville's plan of a grid pattern with every other square left open to serve as a public square. This created a checkerboard of green, public places throughout the town. The planners substituted a diagonal pattern instead of a grid. The city platted the area north of Market Street in 1817 in a grid pattern and without the public squares. Jeffersonville became the county seat of Clark County when the Territorial Assembly created it in 1801. The town served as the county seat until 1812, when Charlestown became the county seat. Jeffersonville became the county seat once again in 1878 and remains the seat of Clark County government.

Civil War

During the American Civil War, Jeffersonville became an important strategic city. Situated directly across from Louisville, Kentucky, it became a staging area for many Union troops going south to fight. Three railroads serviced the city, and of course, it was directly on the Ohio River.

Boat Building Center

Jeffersonville, Indiana became an important boat-building center, stemming from beginnings in 1819 when the first boat building business located there. Steamboats became a very important product of the shipyards there, especially the Howard Shipyards, established in 1834. The company produced the LST landing vehicles during World War 2 and shipbuilding remains an important industry. The Howard Steamboat Museum is dedicated to the ship building industry in Jeffersonville.

The National Register of Historic Places has registered a large portion of the downtown, and the city is working towards restoring and maintaining its historic character. The downtown is populated with popular businesses along the Ohio River Waterfront. Bed and breakfast inns, restaurants, bars, retail stores and public places reside along the River. A visit to Jeffersonville, Indiana would create memories of the place forever.

Tourism Site for Clark and Floyd Counties

Sunny Side of Louisville

Administrative Offices:

315 Southern Indiana Ave.

Jeffersonville, IN 47130

Visitor Center:

305 Southern Indiana Ave.

Jeffersonville, IN 47130

800-552-3842

812-280-5566

Fax: 812-282-1904

tourism@sunnysideoflouisville.org

http://gosoin.com

November 6, 1786 - Isaac Blackford Born

Isaac Blackford (November 6, 1786 – December 31, 1859)

The son of Joseph and Mary Straats Blackford, Isaac was a native of Bound Brook, Somerset County, New Jersey. After receiving a basic education, he enrolled in Princeton University, graduating at the top of his class in 1806. He migrated to the Indiana Territory in 1812 to practice law.

Political and Judicial Career

The voters elected Blackford to the first Indiana General Assembly where he served as the first Speaker of the House of Representatives. Indiana Governor Jonathan Jennings appointed him as Chief Justice of the Indiana Supreme Court in 1817. he would serve in that office until 1853, becoming the longest serving Chief Justice of Indiana and one of the longest serving jurists in the United States. During his tenure, he wrote over 2,000, only 46 of which were overturned. Many consider him the most influential to serve on Indiana's courts. The Constitution of 1851 interrupted his tenure, as it changed the Supreme Court from an appointed position to an elected one. He lost the 1852 nomination. President Franklin Pierce appointed him as a Federal Court Judge on the United States Court of Claims, a position he held until his death in 1859. His body is interred at Crown Hill Cemetery in Indianapolis.

Indiana Colonization Society

Groups promoting emancipation of slaves and supporting colonization of them back to Africa began organizing in Indiana in 1825. The American Colonization Society had formed in 1816 in New Jersey. The group had helped found the country of Liberia on the western coast of Africa to establish these colonies. The ACS encouraged states for form local chapters. The ACS formed out abolitionist groups that wished to end slavery in the United States.

Settlement and Development

The first European settlers moved into the area in the 1830's. These were mostly farmers that settled near the rivers. Most of the county was swampland and as farmers cleared and drained the land, more farmland was suitable for farming. Economic prosperity blossomed when explorers found oil and natural gas in the region.

Hartford City Courthouse Square Historic District

Franklin, Walnut, Water and Mulberry Streets roughly bound the Hartford City Courthouse Square Historic District. There are forty-five historic structures in the district with a mix of retail and public uses. Architecture types include Late Victorian, Italianate, Romanesque, renaissance and art deco. Most of these buildings were erected during the 1879 - 1947 period. The nineteen-acre region was listed on the National Register of Historic Places on June 21, 2006.

Events of 1787

February 11, 1787 - Seth Hinshaw Born

Seth Hinshaw (1787-1865)

A native of Guilford County, North Carolina, Seth was the son of John and Ruth (Pike) Weisner Hinshaw. He and Hannah Beeson married there and together they had five children. The family moved to Henry County, Indiana and settled in Greensboro. While there, he joined the Duck Creek Monthly Meeting of Friends. He also opened his store. By the late 1830's he became involved in the abolitionist movement, becoming active in the Underground Railroad movement. Local legend says that he sheltered black leader Frederick Douglass after a pro-slavery mob attacked him at an abolitionist meeting in Pendleton on September 16, 1843.

He is interred at the Greensboro Friends Cemetery in Greensboro, Indiana.

April 24, 1787 - Congress Appoints Josiah Harmar to Quell Situation at Vincennes

George Rogers Clark's actions in Vincennes and Kaskaskia appeared to present a direct threat to the fledgling United States, so to stabilize the situation, the Confederation Congress appointed General Josiah Harmar to address the situation.

May 25, 1787 - Constitutional Convention Meets - First Time

Weaknesses in the structure of the Articles of Confederation had become apparent as early as 1785, when Maryland and Virginia met to form an agreement that regulated commerce, fishing, and navigation in the waters of the Potomac and Pocomoke Rivers, and Chesapeake Bay. Disputes over payment of debts and confiscated properties owed to former British loyalists led Britain to retain six forts in United States Territory that the Treaty of Paris required them to abandon. These forts included:

Northwest Territory

Fort Miamis in northern Ohio

Fort Mackinac

Fort Lernoult, aka Fort Detroit

New York

Fort Niagara

Fort Oswegatchie

For Ontario

Foment Disorder

The British used many of these outposts, especially Fort Detroit, to foment problems with the natives in the Northwest Territory. Additional problems arose when states attempted to place tariffs on goods imported from other states.

Need for a New Plan

Under the Articles, the United States lacked the power to regulate international trade, impose taxes or even succeed in opening the Spanish blockade of goods passing through New Orleans. The need for a stronger central government became more apparent over time. Finally, the Confederation Congress had authorized a convention to meet and revise the Articles in February 1787.

Delegates Arrive

On May 25, 1787 fifty-five delegates from twelve states met at Independence Hall in Philadelphia, Pennsylvania. Rhode Island declined to attend the convention. The purpose of the convention was to revise the Articles of Confederation. The directive from the Congress stated, " "for the sole and express purpose of revising the Articles of Confederation and reporting to Congress and the several legislatures such alterations and provisions therein and when agreed to in Congress and confirmed by the States render the Federal Constitution adequate to the exigencies of Government and the preservation of the Union."

The Convention Meets

The fifty-five delegates elected George Washington to preside over the convention. The convention met for four months, conducting many debates in secret and affecting numerous compromises to produce the final Constitution in September 1787.

May 29, 1787 - Virginia Plan Presented

Edmund Randolph presented his Virginia Plan for the Constitution to the Convention.

Edmund Randolph (August 10, 1753 – September 12, 1813)

The son of John and Ariana Jenings Randolph, Edmund was native to Tazewell Hall, Williamsburg, Virginia. After attending the College of William and Mary in Williamsburg, Randolph studied law with his father and uncle Peyton.

Revolution Begins

At the outbreak of the American Revolution, his father remained loyal to Britain and migrated to Britain. Edmund joined the Continental Army and served as aide-de-camp to General George Washington. His uncle passed away in October 1775, so Randolph returned to Williamsburg to attend his affairs.

Political Career Begins

While there, he gained election to the Fourth Virginia Convention, which began in December 1775. Several other political positions followed, including mayor of Williamsburg and Virginia's Attorney General of the new government. He and Elizabeth Nicholas married on August 29, 1776. The couple would have six children. He gained election to the 1775 Continental Congress, serving until 1782. In 1786, he became governor of Virginia. As governor, he led a delegation of representatives to the Annapolis Convention in September 1786. The Convention's purpose was to attempt a fix on some of the numerous defects in the Articles of Confederation. Election to the Constitutional Convention followed, where he introduced his Virginia Plan for government to the Positional Convention on May 29, 1787.

Virginia Plan

James Madison probably drafted the Virginia Plan, or variously called the Randolph and Big State Plan, during the early weeks before convention as delegates arrived. Madison never claimed authorship, however most historians believe the document's writing style to be his. He developed the main features of the plan as he corresponded with Thomas Jefferson, Edmund Randolph and George Washington. The Virginia Plan consisted of fifteen resolutions that were debated on the floor during the course of the convention. Even though a written draft of the plan was submitted, the document has been lost to history. The plan featured three branches of government, designed to prevent abuse of power. The plan included a bicameral legislature, an upper house and a lower house. The lower house members would be elected directly by the people and would serve three-year terms. The various state legislatures would select the members of the upper house, who would serve a seven-year term. A state's free population would serve as the base of representatives, with each state's delegates assigned in proportion to their population. Large states with large populations favored this plan, as it would guarantee their dominance in the new government.

May 29, 1787 - Pinckney Plan Presented

South Carolina delegate Charles Pinckney Presented his plan for the new constitution immediately after Randolph concluded introducing his measure.

Charles Pinckney

The son of Charles and Frances Brewton Pinckney, Charles was native to Charleston, South Carolina. During his early years, Dr. David Oliphant tutored him. Oliphant had a huge impact on Pinckney. He taught the boy five languages and imparted his ideas of government, which included the belief that if a government failed its people, those people had the right to form a new one. When he reached maturity, he studied law with his father and gained admittance to the South Carolina bar in 1779. In 1777, at twenty, he gained election to the Continental Congress.

Revolutionary War

Pinckney enlisted in the militia in 1779. His men elected him to serve as lieutenant. During the next year, he and his regiment defended the city during the Siege of Charlestown, which fell on May 12, 1780. The Siege numbers one of the worst defeats suffered by the Americans during the Revolution. The British captured him, but released him after extracting a promise that he would not fight again. They incarcerated him again when the Americans began turning the tide of the conflict against them. Before imprisoning him, the British tried to make him switch sides and fight with them, an offer which he refused. The British released him in June 1779.

After the War

In the years after the war, Pinckney would serve in the Continental Congress and served several terms in the South Carolina Legislature. He became one of the youngest members of the Constitutional Convention when it opened on May 25, 1787.

David Oliphant (1720 - 1805)

Native to Scotland, Oliphant studied medicine there after which he immigrated to South Carolina in 1747. The Continental Congress appointed him as Director-General of Hospitals of the Southern Department on June 1, 1776. The British captured him during the Siege of Charleston, however he received a pardon and he returned to his medical practice. Oliphant gained election to the South Carolina legislature after the war and practiced medicine. Oliphant moved to Newport, Rhode Island, where he died in 1805.

The Pinckney Plan

Historians actually know very little about the plan, as Pinckney did not write it down. The nature of the arrangement included a treaty between the states in which they would form a confederation. Elements included a bicameral legislature composed of a House and Senate. The House members would be elected in proportion to a state's population. The House members would elect members of the Senate. Both houses would meet in joint session to elect a president. There are no records of this plan entering serious debate in the Congress, though it discussed in the Committee of Detail.

May 30, 1787 - Edmund Randolph Proposes Establishing a National Government

The Virginia Plan, presented a day earlier, had begun with the phrase, "Resolved that the Articles of Confederation ought to be so corrected & enlarged as to accomplish the objects proposed by their institution; namely, "common defence, security of liberty and general welfare." Picking up on the theme and the Plan's concept of a national government consisting of three branches, Edmund Randolph proposed that this government should be composed of an executive, judicial and legislative branch. The delegates of the Constitutional Convention quickly agreed to this framework.

June 11, 1787 - Sherman Plan Proposed

Roger Sherman of Connecticut rose to make a simple proposal to the Convention on June 11, 1787.

"That the proportion of suffrage in the 1st. branch should be according to the respective numbers of free inhabitants; and that in the second branch or Senate, each State should have one vote and no more."

Roger Sherman (April 19, 1721 – July 23, 1793)

The son of William and Mehetabel Sweetman Sherman, Roger was native to Newton, Massachusetts. When he was two years old, the family moved to Dorchester (present Stoughton), Massachusetts. Sherman received very little in the way of a formal education. Reading the books in his father's well-stocked library provided the bulk of his learning. He would also read other books when they became available, mostly from a neighbor, the Reverend Samuel Dunbar. For most of his youth, he worked on his father's farm and learned the cobbler trade from him. In 1743, he walked to New Milford, Connecticut. His brother had moved there and Roger joined him in partnership to open a store. Sherman's aptitude for mathematics soon earned him a spot as the county surveyor. In 1754, he read for law and received admittance to the Connecticut bar. Over the next years, he held various political posts including Connecticut Superior Court and stints in both houses of the Connecticut colonial assembly. In 1774, he was elected to the Continental Congress. During the first term, he was one of the signers of the Articles of Association on October 20, 1774. Sherman was also one of the signers of the Declaration of Independence on July 4, 1776 and the Articles of Confederation in 1781. In 1787, he joined Oliver Ellsworth as representatives from Connecticut at the Constitutional Convention.

Proposal Shelved

Sherman and Ellsworth had developed the plan; however, Roger Sherman introduced it. The idea was generally well received, due to the respect the other members of the Convention had for the two men, however the proposal did not receive any serious consideration until July 5.

June 15, 1787 - New Jersey Plan Presented

William Paterson introduced the New Jersey, or Small State Plan.

William Paterson (December 24, 1745 - September 9, 1806)

The son of Richard and Mary Paterson, William was native to Antrim County, Ireland. The Paterson family immigrated to the colonies in 1747, settling first in New Castle, Pennsylvania. The family moved around a great deal until finding their home in Princeton, New Jersey. As a child, Paterson attended private schools and enrolled in the College of New Jersey (Princeton) in 1763. He studied law, gaining his law degree and admittance to the bar in 1768. He opened a practice in New Bromley, New Jersey. Entering politics, Paterson served in several elective posts including delegate and secretary to the Provincial Congress 1775-1776, delegate to the New Jersey Constitutional Convention and New Jersey Attorney General. He resigned the post to move to Raritan, New Jersey. In 1787, voters from his state elected him to the Constitutional Convention in Philadelphia.

New Jersey Plan

Paterson introduced his New Jersey Plan in response to the Virginia Plan, which he opposed. The New Jersey Plan would have amended the Articles of Confederation, not replaced it. The Plan featured a unicameral (one-house) legislature with one member per colony. Under this plan, the Federal Government had the power to use tariffs to generate revenue and regulate disputes between the states. Congress could also impose taxes on the various states. The population of each state determined the tax, based upon the number of free inhabitants and 3/5's of the slave population. Congress also elected the executive council, which consisted of several people. The members of this council would serve one term and could be recalled when a majority of the states demanded that Congress remove them. Federal law was considered the supreme law of the land and the Federal government could force the states to comply. The New Jersey Plan proposed that Congress create a plan to admit new states. It also included a provision that a citizen of one state could be prosecuted for laws broken in another state.

June 18, 1787 - Hamilton Plan Presented

Alexander Hamilton was dissatisfied with both the Virginia and New Jersey plans. On June 18, he presented his own plan that outlined the idea of a strong central government with state sovereignty virtually eliminated. Hamilton based his plan upon the British parliamentary system. The features his plan included:

A bicameral legislature composed of two houses, a Senate and an assembly.

The people would elect the Assembly for a term of three years

The Congress would divide the nation into election districts that did not necessarily adhere to state lines. One Senator would be elected per district and would serve for life.

People in the election districts mentioned beforehand would choose electors who would then choose the governor to serve over the United States. This governor would serve for life, unless removed by the legislature. His powers included:

Veto power over all laws passed by the Legislature

Served as commander in chief of military forces in any war declared by the Legislature

Power to appoint Federal department heads

Power to pardon people for everything but treason, which he needed approval of the Senate to grant

The Senate's powers included:

The power to declare war

Advise and consent to all department heads appointed by the Governor

Advise and consent on all treaties

The Legislature had the power to institute courts and appoint judges in each of the states

The courts had the power to impeach Federal officials

The Legislature had the power to appoint the governors of each state

This governor had veto power over any law passed by the state legislature

All laws passed by the state legislature that were contrary to Federal law were voided

No state had the power to maintain any military force of any kind

Final Constitution Included Some of Hamilton's Ideas

The other delegates studied Hamilton's plan and considered it well thought out. However, few, if any, considered it as a plan for the United States, as it was too similar to the monarchial system of Great Brittan, a system they had spent nearly a decade of war throwing off. Some of the features of Hamilton's plan did make it into the final draft of the Constitution.

June 20, 1787 - Oliver Ellsworth Proposed the Name United States

Connecticut delegate Oliver Ellsworth raised an objection to using the phrase "national government," in the document on which the convention labored.

Oliver Ellsworth (April 29, 1745 – November 26, 1807)

The son of David and Jemima Leavitt Ellsworth, Oliver was native to Windsor, Connecticut. He enrolled in Yale College in 1762, however the next year he transferred to College of New Jersey (Princeton). He graduated with an AB Degree in 1766. Two years later, he began studying law, gaining admittance to the bar in 1771. The next year he married Abigail Wolcott, with whom he had nine children. He opened a law practice and politics, gaining the office of State Attorney for Hartford County in Connecticut in 1777. That same year he became one of Connecticut's delegates to the Continental Congress. In addition to this, he became a member of the forerunner of the Supreme Court, the Committee of Appeals. His service in the Continental Congress ran to six consecutive annual terms. He was elected to join the Constitutional Convention in Philadelphia in 1787, along with two other delegates from Connecticut, Roger Sherman and William Samuel Johnson.

The Name Change

Ellsworth believed that reference to the government the delegates worked to create, as a national government would work to destroy the states, which would destroy the union. He preferred the term "United States," as a union of the states was they wished to accomplish. He reasoned that they should send the finished document to the various state legislatures for ratification, not to the people as a whole. His worry was that if they allowed the people to vote on it, then it would be hard to avoid later conventions, which might upset the union they sought to create. If they sent it to the states, the process to call conventions would be harder, thus rarer. In fact, the delegates never considered sending the document out to the people for ratification; they always sought to have a plurality of the states ratify the document. The name "United States," had been used before on several documents, including the Declaration of Independence, thus it was a familiar name. Ellsworth's proposal passed the Convention and the name of the new entity became the United States.

July 02, 1787 - Grand Committee Appointed

By early July, an impasse had developed in the Congress. On June 19, the Convention had discarded the New Jersey Plan in favor of the Virginia Plan. Oliver Ellsworth had made a proposal for equal representation for the states in the Congress. However, large states objected to the equal representation the Ellsworth's proposal outlined. Small state objected to proportional representation in the chambers, fearing that large states with larger population would dominate this assembly. They favored Ellsworth's proposal, in which all states had equal representation. Thus, the debate became small state versus large state. On July 2, the Convention held a vote to accept one vote per state representation. The vote resulted in five states for, five states against and one state divided on the issue.

States in favor:

Connecticut, New York, New Jersey, Delaware, and Maryland

States against the proposal:

Massachusetts, Pennsylvania, Virginia, North Carolina, and South Carolina

With the impasse, many states threatened to withdraw from the convention, thus dooming its goal of replacing the Articles of Confederation with a better plan. With the convention's continuation hanging in the balance, the Pinckney's from South Carolina suggested appointing a committee to resolve the crises. The delegates agreed to form a committee composed of one delegate from each colony to come up with a compromise plan. The committee members were:

Abraham Baldwin (GA)

Gunning Bedford (DE)

William Davie (NC)

Oliver Ellsworth (CT)

Benjamin Franklin (PA)

Elbridge Gerry (MA)

Luther Martin (MD)

George Mason (VA)

William Paterson (NJ)

John Rutledge (SC)

Robert Yates (NY)

The delegates would meet over the Fourth of July weekend and report their progress the following week. Eldridge Gerry would chair the committee.

Oliver Ellsworth had become ill and did not attend. Roger Sherman took his place at the deliberations.

July 05, 1787 Gerry Committee Report

After two days of adjournment while the Grand Committee deliberated, the Congress convened on July 5, 1787. Their report included the following recommendations:

1. The legislative branch would have two chambers.

2. Representation in First Branch by population (1:40,000).

3. Representation in the Second Branch would give each State an equal vote.

4. Money Bills to originate in First Branch and not subject to amendment in Second Branch.

July 7, 1787 - Harmar Departs Falls of the Ohio for Vincennes

The plan to bring the Vincennes area under the control of the United States and expel Clark began when General Josiah Harmar sent Captain Ziegler down the Ohio River towards the mouth of the Wabash on July 6.

The Army on the Move

Captain Ziegler commanded sixty men on eleven boats that included keelboats and canoes laden with the bulk of the expedition's supplies. General Josiah Harmar had been stationed in the Falls of the Ohio River area to protect the area around the falls. Harmar's force consisted of over 1000 men. The flotilla of supplies and Harmar's army rendezvoused on the north bank of the river at a place called the "rocks," which is in current Warrick County about eight miles upstream from the spot where the Green River empties into the Ohio from Kentucky. They landed at this spot on July 10. On July 11, Harmar put Major John F. Hamtramck in command of the supply boats and 300 soldiers, and dispatched them down the river. Harmar, meanwhile, marched from the Ohio overland through a land covered heavily with thickets and bereft of water to catch the Vincennes Trace. At that point, they would continue marching west to Vincennes.

July 16, 1787 - Connecticut Compromise Approved by Committee

After several days of debate, approving various resolutions and rejecting others, the Congress had achieved major progress on several fronts. They had set the number of representatives to the lower house at 65, agreed on taking a census of the population in order to apportion the lower house correctly at one representative for each 40,000 people.

By July 16, the delegates voted on the proposal the Gerry Committee had introduced on July 5.

Connecticut Compromise

The delegates approved the proposal, known variously as the Connecticut Compromise, Sherman Compromise or Great Compromise, on Monday, July 16. Sherman's proposal, made almost a month earlier and largely ignored, had saved the Congress and laid an important step in establishing the Constitution of the United States.

July 13, 1787 - Northwest Territory Ordinance Adopted

Congress established the Northwest Territory on July 13, 1787. The Territory existed as a legal entity from that date until Ohio became a State in 1803. Congress eventually carved six states out of the Territory.

July 17, 1787 - Harmar Arrives Vincennes

General Josiah Harmar and his troops arrived in Vincennes on July 17, 1787.

Clark Departed

By the time Harmar arrived in Vincennes on July 17, Clark had departed from Vincennes during the spring and had left a detachment of troops commanded by Captain Valentine Thomas Dalton in command. Dalton's troops, with no outside support, had been making "tomahawk grants," in the lands around Vincennes and creating other problems for the Vincennes residents. Congress had established the Northwest Territory, but had made no provision for governing the vast area, thus Harmar and his Army troops provided the only law in the territory. Harmar found that Dalton and the remainder of Clark's force had already left the area. Harmar probably first ensconced himself and his troops in the old Fort Patrick Henry, but found the fort unusable because the water supply was unsuitable. Thus, Harmar moved his camp about a quarter of a mile upstream and made their new camp on the banks of the Wabash. In August, Harmar traveled to Kaskaskia and other former French towns on the Mississippi River now under American jurisdiction. He returned to Vincennes by September 3 and two days later entertained a delegation of Piankeshaw Indians. During his tenure, he issued a declaration regarding land ownership in the territory and had numerous meetings with the inhabitants, mostly on similar topics. On October 1, Harmar departed for the fort at the Falls of the Ohio, leaving Major Jean François Hamtramck in command of the post.

July 23, 1787 – Constitutional Convention Agrees to Submit Constitution to Special State Conventions

After rejecting a proposal to send the completed constitution to the state legislatures for ratification, the delegates voted to allow the people of the various states elect delegates for a special convention. These delegates would attend a convention in their states for the purpose of ratifying, or rejecting, the constitution. The vote was 9 - 1 in favor of the proposal.

July 24, 1787 - Committee of Detail Appointed to Write First Draft of Constitution

The Convention's delegates appointed five men to write the first draft of the Constitution:

John Rutledge

Edmund J. Randolph

Nathaniel Gorham

Oliver Ellsworth

James Wilson

The convention adjourned on July 26 and remained in recess until August 7 while the men labored to provide the first written copy of the Constitution of the United States.

August 06, 1787 - Constitutional Convention Reconvenes

The Convention convened long enough to receive the Committee of Details Report, and then promptly adjourned so the members could read the twenty-three article document.

September 15, 1787 - Constitutional Convention Approves the United States Constitution

On Saturday, September 15, 1787, the delegates of the Constitutional Convention in Philadelphia approved the document they had spent months devising by a unanimous vote, 10 - 0.

September 17, 1787 - Constitutional Convention Adjourns

The delegates convened for one last session on Monday, September 17, 1787. After a brief discussion in which a couple of minor changes were made, the document was read aloud to the forty-one assembled documents.

Randolph Predicts Failure

At the conclusion of the reading, Edmund J. Randolph predicted, "Nine states will fail to ratify the plan and confusion must ensue."

Rising Sun

Ben Franklin, who had observed a painting of a rising sun that resided on the wall behind the President's Chair, gave a brief speech, "Painters had found it difficult to distinguish in their art a rising from a setting sun. I have said he, often and often in the course of the Session, and the vicissitudes of my hopes and fears as to its issue, looked at that behind the President without being able to tell whether it was rising or setting: But now at length I have the happiness to know that it is a rising and not a setting Sun."

Signing the Document

At the conclusion of Franklin's brief oratory, the delegates rose to sign the document. Only forty-one of the original fifty-five remained. Three would refrain signing what they considered a deeply flawed document. Thus, the Constitution contains the signatures of thirty-eight delegates, sixteen of whom would go on to become United States Senators.

Convention Adjourns

Their work concluded; the Convention adjourned for the last time. Most of the delegates went to the City Tavern to enjoy one last meal together before disbursing to their various states.

A copy of each document was then sent out to each of the states. The battle for ratification had begun.

October 03, 1787 - Major John Hamtramck Appointed Commander of Vincennes

General Josiah Harmar placed Major Jean François Hamtramck in charge of the Vincennes post on October 3, 1787, ordering him to build a fort at the site.

Major Jean François Hamtramck (August 14, 1756 – April 11, 1803)

The son of Charles-David Hamtramck and Marie-Ann Bertin, Jean was native to Montreal, New France. Historians know little of his early life until he migrated to the United States at the beginning of the Revolutionary War to enlist in the Continental Army. He changed his name to John at this time. He served as a commissary officer, which is an officer that was in charge of gathering and distributing food supplies to the army. His exemplary performance of his duties brought a steady rise in rank to Captain and then to Brevet Major at the end of the war. He left the army, returning in 1785 to serve under General Harmar in the posts along the Ohio River.

Fort Knox I

Hamtramck had his troops construct the fort near the town of Vincennes, naming it Fort Knox, after the Secretary of War at the time, Henry Knox. At the time, Fort Knox was the army's most western post. It was the third fort constructed in Vincennes. The first, known under various names the most common being Fort Vincennes, was built in 1731 by François Marie Besot, Sieur de Vincennes. Lieutenant Governor Edward Abbott rebuilt this fort in 1777 when he took over command of the fort. George Rogers Clark had renamed this fort, Fort Patrick Henry when he captured it in 1779. The

George Rogers Clark National Memorial currently occupies the site of this fort on the south side of Vincennes. By 1787, this fort had fallen into disrepair. Hamtrampk built his fort at another site, currently marked by an historical marker at the corner of Buntin & 1st Streets in Vincennes. Fort Knox I would be occupied until 1803, when it was moved to a site about two miles north of Vincennes.

October 05, 1787, General Arthur St. Clair Chosen Governor of Northwest Territory

The Confederation Congress chose the President of the Congress, Arthur St. Clair, as governor of the Northwest Territory.

Arthur St. Clair (March 23, 1737– August 31, 1818)

A native of Thurso, Caithness, Scotland, historians are uncertain of the identity of St. Clair's parentage or his early life. In 1757, he purchased a commission in the Royal Army. The Army assigned him to serve under General Jeffrey Amherst in Canada. During the French and Indian War, he participated in the battle at Louisburg and the Battle of the Plains of Abraham. At the conclusion of the war, he resigned his commission and migrated to the Ligonier Valley, Pennsylvania. There, he became a major landowner and held several political posts.

Revolutionary War

When war broke out between England and her colonies, St. Clair took a commission as a colonel of the 3rd Pennsylvania Regiment. During the war, he participated in the Battle of Trois-Rivières, the Battle of Trenton and at the capture of Princeton, New Jersey. Many believe St. Clair provided the strategy for Washington's victory over the British there. Washington put him in charge at Fort Ticonderoga. His controversial decision to abandon that strategic fort caused his court-martial in 1778. The court exonerated him, but he would receive no more commands during the remainder of the war. Washington retained his confidence and installed him as his aide-de-camp, a position he held until the end of the war.

Pennsylvania Delegate to Confederation Congress

In 1785, he gained election to the Confederation Congress. The delegates of the Congress elected him President of the Congress in February 1787, a position he held when the Congress passed the Northwest Territory Ordinance in 1787.

Governor of Northwest Territory

Congress appointed St. Clair as governor of the Northwest Territory, a position he held concurrently with his office of President until his term as president expired on November 4, 1787. He would establish the capital of the Northwest Territory initially at Marietta, Ohio. Later the capital would move to Cincinnati, Ohio. He would serve as Territorial Governor of first the Northwest Territory, then the Ohio Territory until 1802.

1787 – Seth Hinshaw Born

Seth Hinshaw (1787-1865)

A native of Guilford County, North Carolina, Seth was the son of John and Ruth (Pike) Weisner Hinshaw. He and Hannah Beeson married there and together they had five children. The family moved to Henry County, Indiana and settled in Greensboro. While there, he joined the Duck Creek Monthly Meeting of Friends. He also opened his store. By the late 1830's he became involved in the abolitionist movement, becoming active in the Underground Railroad movement. Local legend says that he sheltered black leader Frederick Douglass after a pro-slavery mob attacked him at an abolitionist meeting in Pendleton on September 16, 1843.

He is interred at the Greensboro Friends Cemetery in Greensboro, Indiana.

The Indiana Historical Society maintains a marker at the corner of Main Street and Greensboro Pike in Greensboro, Henry County.

Title of Marker:

Underground Station

Location:

SE corner Main Street & Greensboro Pike, Greensboro. (Henry County, Indiana)

Installed by:

Erected by Greensboro Women's Auxiliary and Greensboro Corporation

Marker ID #:

33.1976.1

Marker Text:

Seth Hinshaw, (1787-1865), well-known abolitionist, operated a station of the Underground Railroad on this site, prior to the Civil War. He also operated a store in which he refused to sell goods produced by slave labor. In 1843, Hinshaw helped erect Liberty Hall, which was located one block west of this site, where many fiery anti-slavery meetings were held under his direction.

Note: A Report by the Indiana Historical Bureau states that most of the information on the marker is correct, very little is verified. This is because the people that engaged in the activities were conducting illegal acts and kept few records. The report indicates that more research is needed to verify. For information about this report, click this link.

http://www.in.gov/history/files/33.1976.1_Underground_ Station_Final.pdf

Events of 1788

April 07, 1788 - Marietta, Ohio Established - First Seat of Northwest Territory Government

The Ohio Company of Associates purchased 1.5 million acres of land along the Ohio River in the region that would become Ohio in 1788, planning to use the land to pay Revolutionary War veterans. Revolutionary War veteran Rufus Putnam led a group of forty-eight men to settle in this tract of land. They landed on April 7, 1788 at the mouth of the Muskingum River. They founded Marietta, Ohio at the site, which became the first capital of the Northwest Territory a few months later.

The new settlement was on the opposite side of the Muskingum River from Fort Harmar, established three years earlier.

April 10, 1788 - William Paul Quinn Born

Harrison County, Indiana has had a black population since Territorial days. The Northwest Ordinance prohibited slavery, but the local officials tolerated it. Thus, the 1810 census lists twenty-one slaves and several free persons of color. In 1814, a group of about 100 blacks migrated in accompanied by their white benefactors, Paul and Susannah Mitchem. These blacks settled around Harrison County and became farmers and merchants. Many of these blacks and their descendents were involved in the St. Paul African Methodist Episcopal Church.

William Paul Quinn (April 10, 1788 - February 21, 1873)

A native of Hindustan, India, which is near Calcutta, Quinn is of Indian descent. Exposed to the Quaker faith, he converted and suffered ostracism in his native land. He migrated to England and finally to New York in 1806. He joined an anti-slavery sect of Quakers known as the

Hicksites. Elias Hicks, a Quaker abolitionist activist, founded the group. He later converted to the Methodist faith in 1808 while visiting Missouri on a mission. The Methodists licensed him as a minister in 1812 and was one of the African Methodist Episcopal (AME) Church's founders in 1816. He began as a circuit preacher in New Jersey, but in 1836, the church assigned him to the "Western Mission." The church elected him bishop on May 19, 1844. As bishop, a post he held for twenty-five years, he helped establish forty-seven new churches across the nation, the bulk of them in the American Midwest. He died in Richmond, Indiana on February 21, 1873.

The Indiana Historical Bureau has installed an historical marker in Corydon, honoring Quinn:

Title of Marker:

St. Paul African Methodist Episcopal Church

Location:

SE corner of Maple & High streets, Corydon. (Harrison County, Indiana)

Installed by:

2003 Indiana Historical Bureau and St. Paul's A.M.E. Building Fund Organization

Marker ID #:

31.2003.1

Marker Text:

Side one:

Free blacks and former slaves organized an African Methodist Episcopal congregation in Corydon by 1843. In 1851, church trustees purchased land in Corydon in order to build a church and for school purposes. In 1878, church trustees purchased land at this site and later built a frame church.

Side two:

In August 1975, the congregation dedicated the brick church adjacent to this site. William Paul Quinn, appointed A.M.E. missionary 1840, established many congregations in frontier Indiana; elected Bishop 1844. Many early churches served as schools and enriched black social, cultural, and political life

July 09, 1788 - General St. Clair Arrives Marietta

General Arthur St. Clair arrived in the new settlement of Marietta, in the Northwest Territory, to begin his administration as governor of the Territory. The capital remained in Marietta until 1790, when St. Clair moved it to Cincinnati. St. Clair used Fort Harmar as his headquarters.

July 26, 1788 - Washington County Established - Northwest Territory

Northwest Territorial Governor Arthur St. Clair established the territory's first county, Washington, by decree on July 26, 1788. He named the new county after General George Washington.

February 22, 1732 - George Washington Born

Augustine Washington and his second wife, Mary Ball Washington celebrated the birth of their first son, George at their Pope's Creek Estate on February 11, 1732. The switchover from the Julian calendar to the Gregorian calendar by the British Empire moved his birthday to February 22, 1732. Augustine was a moderately successful tobacco farmer, considered "middling gentry." He had three children from his first marriage to Jane Butler Washington, who died in 1729. Augustine married Mary Ball in 1731. Six of Washington's half siblings survived to adulthood. These included his half brothers Lawrence and Augustine. Four of his full siblings survived childhood, Samuel, Elizabeth (Betty), John Augustine and Charles.

Death of Augustine

George's father died suddenly in 1743, when George was eleven years old. His older half-brother Lawrence became a surrogate father to him. At his father's death, George inherited Ferry Farm, where he spent most of his childhood. Historians know little of Washington's early years. His father's death made it impossible for him to attend England's Appleby School, where his older siblings had gone. Instead he was home-schooled, tutored and attended a nearby school run by an Anglican minister. He considered joining the Royal Navy, but his mother objected. George dropped the idea.

Surveyor

George trained as a surveyor and at age, sixteen he traveled with a surveyor party into western Virginia. When he was seventeen, Lord Fairfax helped him gain appointment as the official surveyor of Culpeper County. For two years, he surveyed the wild lands of western Virginia. The experience taught him much about living on the frontier. It toughened both his body and mind to weather conditions and exposed him to the frontier wisdom of the pioneers he met. The generous pay also enabled him to purchase prime land in Virginia, extending his holdings.

Exposure to Virginia Governor Robert Dinwiddie

His position and his brother's rank in the Virginia militia brought him into contact with Virginia Dinwiddie, who was suitably impressed with the six foot tall George Washington, who towered over his contemporaries. It was a fateful, for Washington and the American colonies, association.

Dinwiddie's confidence in the young Washington would form a crucial plank in the young man's development into a leader.

October 31, 1753- Washington Sent on Mission to Assess French Strength in Ohio Valley

The rivalry between the French and English in North America in the years before the French and Indian War created the opportunity for a youthful George Washington to gain experience in military matters. Both the French and the English had claimed the vast Ohio River Valley region.

Dinwiddie Becomes Concerned

The French had established colonies along the St. Lawrence River in Canada and at the mouth of the Mississippi River in Louisiana. They desired the Ohio River Valley region so they could connect the two regions by water. In 1749, the French had sent Pierre-Joseph Celeron de Blainville on the Lead Plate Expedition. Blainville had buried lead or copper plates at the mouths of all the major rivers they encountered on their route down the Allegheny, Ohio and Mississippi Rivers. By the early 1750, the French began building a string of forts in the region to establish control. The forts were, in order of their establishment, Fort Presque Isle, Fort Leboef and Fort Machault along the Allegheny River. Their actions created friction with the British. Royal charters granted to Virginia and other colonies had extended their claims from the eastern seaboard to the Pacific Ocean. Virginia Governor Robert Dinwiddie had extensive real estate holdings in the Ohio River Valley region. French and British fur traders quarreled over trading rights with the natives. The Ohio Company, to which George Washington had ties, had also begun exploring the area. The conflicting claims led to increasing tensions between the two powerful nations.

Washington Given an Important Mission

Dinwiddie had sent one mission to the region that fell 150 miles short of reaching their goal of Fort Le Boeuf in northwest Pennsylvania. He had heard of George Washington and suspected he might be up to the task of completing the arduous mission. He contacted Washington and instructed him to go to Willis Creek (Maryland), where the Ohio Company maintained a supply warehouse. He was to hire Christopher Gist to use as a guide and then procure porters to carry the goods. Dinwiddie had written a letter to the French commander of Fort Le Boeuf, demanding that the French halt their incursions into the area. Washington's orders further stated that, after he had acquired supplies and porters, he was to proceed to Logstown, an Amerindian settlement along the Ohio River to hold council with the natives living there.

Washington traveled to Willis Creek as instructed and gathered his men and supplies. On October 31, 1753, George Washington set off on his first important military mission.

November 24, 1753 - Washington Reaches Forks of the Ohio

After nearly a month of wilderness travel, George Washington and his company arrived at the Forks of the Ohio. They had accomplished nearly half of their journey to the French Fort Le Boeuf.

Forks of the Ohio

Washington's military mind surveyed the area of the forks and reached a favorable impression of the site. He noted in his journal that a fort at the forks would dominate the three rivers and offer a strong defense of the Monongahela River. The Monongahela was smooth, deep, and navigable. It had its source in Virginia. He also noted that the Monongahela and the Allegheny River formed a nearly right angle at the junction and that the area above the rivers was about twenty-five feet above the water. The rivers were each about a quarter of a mile wide, at that point. The land around the proposed fort was well timbered, flat and ideal for a fortification.

From the Forks, Washington and his party continued on to their destination, Fort Le Boeuf.

November 30, 1753 - Washington Departs from Logstown

Colonel Washington's journey to Fort Le Boeuf took him to Logstown, an important Amerindian village along the Ohio River in western Pennsylvania.

Logstown

Originally settled by the Shawnee around 1725 on a site about eighteen miles below the junction of the Allegheny and Monongahela Rivers, the site became an important settlement. The French had built over thirty log cabins in the village for the natives in 1747 in an attempt to woo them to their side in their growing conflict with the British. An important trading site, the Mingo, Shawnee and Delaware tribes all had representatives in the town.

Washington's Arrival

Washington arrived in Logstown on November 24 with hopes of conferring with several of the natives and aligning them with the British. He presented gifts to the Seneca half king, Tanaghrisson, who was in charge of the town. Tanaghrisson seemed eager at first to ally with the British and send a delegation to accompany Washington to Fort Le Boeuf. He claimed it would take a few days to prepare for the journey, an inconvenience that did not please the impatient Washington. When they finally departed on November 30, Washington was disappointed that the native delegation included only several old chiefs and a warrior that would provide them with fresh meat.

December 04, 1753 - Washington Reaches Fort Venango

Washington's expedition reached Fort Venango in northwestern Pennsylvania near present day Franklin, Pennsylvania on December 4, 1753. The French had expelled British fur trader John Frasier from his trading post earlier. The French commander was in the process of transforming the trading post into a fort. The commander refused to accept Washington's letter from Dinwiddie and recommended that he continue on to Fort Le Boeuf.

December 11, 1753 - Washington Arrives at Fort Le Boeuf

Major George Washington had departed from Willis Creek in Maryland on October 31, 1754, carrying a letter from Virginia Governor Robert Dinwiddie. Washington had arrived at the French fort Venango on December 4. His effort to deliver the letter from Dinwiddie had been rebuffed by the commander of that fort, who sent him on to Fort Le Boeuf. He arrived at his destination on December 11, 1754. The next day he presented his letter to the French commander of the fort, Jacques Legardeur de Saint-Pierre. Legardeur at first wanted to send Washington on to Quebec to the French governor, however Washington refused, insisting that Legardeur take it.

Jacques Legardeur de Saint-Pierre (October 24, 1701 - September 8, 1755)

The son of Jean-Paul Legardeur de Saint-Pierre and Marie-Josette Leneuf de La Vallière, Jean-Paul was native to Montreal. Legardeur's father had made a career in the military, and Jean-Paul decided upon that road himself. He received the rank of second ensign in 1724. During his career, he gained a reputation as a master of strong-arm diplomacy. Legardeur rose steadily in the ranks and served as commandant of several French military posts. He had become the commander of Fort Le Boeuf in 1753. After his meeting with Washington, Legardeur served in the French and Indian War, dying at the Battle of Lac Saint-Sacrement in 1755.

Refusal

Legardeur took two days to deliver a reply to Washington. During this time, Washington did not sit idly by. He spent his time assessing the strength of the fort and gathering whatever other intelligence he could. After two days, Legardeur refused Dinwiddie's demand that the French vacate the Ohio River Valley. They would continue building forts and would not relinquish their claims to the region. Washington received Legardeur's letter and began his long, difficult return to Virginia.

December 27, 1753 - George Washington and Christopher Gist Ambushed By Indians

On the return from their mission to Fort Le Boeuf during the French and Indian War, Washington and Gist passed through Murdering Town in Pennsylvania. Murdering Town, or as some call it Murthering Town, was a Lenape village located along the Venango Path, which ran from the Forks of the Ohio to Presque Isle. A few miles south of the village, an Indian who had allied himself to the French shot an arrow, narrowly missing Washington. Historians do not know the exact location, however a stone marker near Evans City, denotes the most likely spot.

December 29, 1753 - Washington Crosses Frozen Allegheny River on Raft

George Washington's most famous river crossing was during the Revolutionary War when he crossed the Delaware River as he maneuvered his troops in the hours before his victory at Trenton, New Jersey. His first river crossing in a hastily built raft took place almost twenty-three years before while on his first important diplomatic mission to the French prior to the French and Indian War.

Bitter Cold Weather

George Washington's party of seven had completed their journey to Fort Le Boeuf on the banks of Le Boeuf Creek in northwestern Pennsylvania. By December 13, the French commander had given a letter to Washington in reply to the Virginia governor's request that French forces leave the Ohio River Valley. He had denied the request. Washington was anxious to get the negative news back to the governor and had departed immediately. The weather turned cold, snowy and windy. Heavy snow and bitter cold impeded their progress. The horses, tired and overburdened with supplies, made slow progress in the snow. His exhausted men, frostbitten and weary, could scarcely walk. On December 25, Washington decided to go ahead with his bad news, leaving five men of the expedition to return with the horses and supplies as the weather allowed. He chose his guide, Christopher Gist, as his companion for the journey. The two traveled by night to avoid detection by the natives. They were detected once and a native fired on them, narrowly missing Washington.

Icy Crossing

The men arrived at the Allegheny River near the site of present day Pittsburg on December 28 after a forty-mile walk in the snow and cold. Washington could only have felt dismay when he saw the river. He had expected that the cold weather would have frozen it, allowing him and Gist to cross over the ice. However, it was not frozen. The swollen current carried huge chunks of ice with it as it swept by the nearly frozen men. Determined to cross, the men spent December 29 building a raft. The only tool the men had was a hatchet. With this, they cut logs and vines, fashioning their raft. By night, they had finished. In the darkness, they pushed the raft into the frigid water and started across the treacherous waters. By the time they reached midstream, the raft became jammed in ice flows. Washington wrote later in his journal:

"Before we were half way over, we were jammed in the ice in such a manner that we expected every minute to perish. I put out my setting pole to stop the raft, and the rapidity of the stream jerked me out into 10 feet of water, but I saved myself by catching hold of one of the raft logs. With all our efforts, we could not get to either shore, but I was obliged, as we were near an island, to quit our raft and make it."

The two men spent a wet, cold night on that island. By morning the river had frozen. Gist and Washington walked across the frozen surface.

Washington Crossing Bridge

The island Washington and Gist spent the night on has long since disappeared. It lay between current 38th and 40th Streets in Philadelphia. The Washington Crossing Bridge on 40th Street, built in 1924, is named in honor of the men's feat.

January 16, 1754 - Washington Arrives Back at Williamsburg

George Washington completed his harrowing Allegheny Expedition when he returned to Williamsburg on January 16, 1754. Washington presented both his journal and the letter containing the French reply to Dinwiddie's demand to Governor Robert Dinwiddie. Washington had completed his first major assignment. Concerned about French incursion into the Ohio River Valley, Dinwiddie began immediately to prepare a force to construct a fort at the Forks of the Ohio.

May 28, 1754 - Battle of Jumonville Glen - Sets off French and Indian War

All wars have to have a beginning point somewhere. Most historians regard the Battle of Jumonville Glenn as the opening battle of the Seven Years War, known as the French and Indian War in North America. George Washington played a central role in this battle.

Jockeying for Dominance

The French and the British both claimed the rich region of the Ohio River Valley. The Amerindian inhabitants that lived in the region shifted alliances between the two powers, depending upon which offered them the better bargain for their alliance. By the early part of the decade, their allegiance began to shift towards the British. However, it was a tenuous shift. When Virginia Royal Governor Robert Dinwiddie had sent George Washington on his mission to warn the French to leave the Ohio River Valley Region in October 1753, Washington had passed through the Forks of the Ohio area on his way to Fort Le Boeuf. The area had impressed him as an ideal place to build a fort. Thus, when Dinwiddie had wanted to fortify the area, he acted upon his trusted colonial officer's recommendation and ordered Captain William Trent and a company of colonial militia to build a fort at the site. Trent had arrived in mid-February and began constructing the fort the British would call Fort Prince George.

Dinwiddie Orders Reinforcements and a Road

In March 1754, Dinwiddie ordered Washington to gather a force together to reinforce Trent's company at Fort Prince George and begin building a road. Washington complied, departing for the area by April 2, 1754 with 160 men. More militia joined him at Winchester. Unknown to Dinwiddie and Washington a French force of 500 - 600 soldiers had arrived at Fort Prince George on April 17 and forced Trent, with his far smaller force, to leave. The French tore down Fort Prince George and began construction of the larger Fort Duquesne. Upon informing Washington of these developments, Trent joined Washington's force to return to the Forks of the Ohio region to build the road Dinwiddie wanted.

Fort Necessity

Washington's force had built the road to an area called Great Meadows, a marshy clearing in the forest, by May 14. He built a base camp here to store supplies. Then he began sending out scout parties to explore the area while waiting for Dinwiddie to send more troops. One of the scouting parties led by Washington's companion on the December mission to Fort Le Boeuf, Robert Gist, discovered that a French scouting party was operating in the area. One of Washington's native allies, a Mingo chief named Tanacharison (Half King), suggested that Washington should lead a force to ambush the party.

Battle of Jumonville Glen

Because of the tenuous relationship between the natives and the British, Washington agreed, to retain support of the chief. Various accounts of the battle that followed blur many of the details. By one account, Washington's force of about seventy-five men surrounded the French force, numbering about forty. Shots were fired and a battle of about fifteen minutes ensued. Washington prevailed, his men killing about ten of the French and forcing the surrender of the remainder. After the surrender, Tanacharison allegedly walked up to the commander of the French party, Joseph Coulon de Villiers de Jumonville, and struck him in the head. The blow killed the officer. This act would play a major role in the war that followed. Washington fell back to Fort Necessity and began reinforcing the structure.

The stage was set for Washington's first, and only, battlefield defeat at the July 4, 1754 Battle of Great Meadows.

June 3, 1754 - Lieutenant Colonel George Washington Completes Construction of Fort Necessity

George Washington knew that the Virginian's victory over the French force at the Battle of Jumonville Glen would lead to a retaliatory strike.

Withdrawal to Great Meadows

After the battle, Washington withdrew his troops to Great Meadows. He built a small stockade on the site to store supplies. This fort was small, only fifty-three feet in diameter with seven-foot tall walls. It had a hut in the middle for storage of gunpowder and other supplies. He did not intend as a defensive position, only as a storage facility. He intended to move on to another spot, called Red Stone Creek, some distance away. Once he completed construction of the fort, he would spend the next month trying to convince some native tribes in the region to help him. He also had the road widened and continued on towards Red Stone Creek while he awaited reinforcements from Virginia.

July 4, 1754 - George Washington Surrenders Fort Necessity to France

The Battle of Great Meadows slapped young Lieutenant Colonel George Washington with his first, and only, battlefield surrender.

Inexperience as Commander

This campaign was Washington's first experience wielding a military force. After his men finished construction, he realized that Fort Necessity was in a bad position. It occupied boggy soil in the center of a depression. His men had only cut the tree line back about a hundred yards. At that range, the besieging French troops could hide in the forest and fire on the fort from cover. They could also charge downhill. He did not have time to rectify his mistake. French commander Louis Coulon de Villiers led the French troops.

At the earlier Battle of Jumonville Glen, an Indian killed his younger brother, Ensign Joseph Coulon de Villiers, during Washington's interrogation. Louis considered the death a murder and wanted vengeance.

British Reinforcements

Under orders from his superior, Washington's men had built a road through the wilderness. The road would allow reinforcing troops to move towards the area. This road did help the reinforcing forces arrive. On June 9, the remainder of the Virginia Militia Regiment arrived, followed by 100 British regular troops a week later. Washington's force now numbered about 400 men and nine swivel guns. On June 16, Washington led 300 of his men out of Fort Necessity to continue work on the road. He needed it for the additional reinforcements he believed would arrive. His intelligence from Fort Duquesne led him to believe that there were only 500 French troops there. He felt that these had inferior training. After the Battle of Jumonville Glen, Washington's native allies had largely deserted him. He needed those reinforcements badly.

Retreat to Fort Necessity

Some of the natives did continue to supply Washington with intelligence about French movements. From these reports, he decided to retreat to Fort Necessity. The troops arrived back there on July 1, 1754. The militia began work improving the defensive works around the fort and enlarging the perimeter. They attempted to dig defensive trenches, but these quickly filled with water in the boggy soil.

The Arrival of the French

On July 3, six hundred French troops and one hundred native warriors arrived. They occupied the forests surrounding Fort Necessity. They had used the road Washington's troops had painstakingly cut through the forest. The occupied the high ground around the fort and poured a relentless fire into it. The attack continued throughout the day. Washington's causalities mounted. A pouring rain arrived, wetting the gunpowder. His situation dire, Washington remembered the ferocity of the Indians he had seen in battle. There were over a hundred warriors among the besiegers. His military career might just be ending.

Faulty Intelligence

Louis Coulon de Villiers received a report that a large British force was closing in on the site. It was a false report, but de Villiers could not know this. De Villiers did not wish to be caught by vengeful British troops. If they discovered a massacre at the fort, or his men herding a line of prisoners, it could be fatal. De Villiers sent messengers to the besieged Washington in the late evening. He offered to allow Washington and his troops to depart the fort unharmed. The negotiations took a lot of time, as de Villiers did not speak English and Washington spoke no French. They soon consummated a deal and on the morning of July 4, 1754, Washington signed the agreement. Since Washington could not read French, he was not aware that de Villiers had inserted a clause in the agreement. In this clause, Washington admitted to the murder of Ensign Joseph Coulon de Villiers while a prisoner of war. The French would use this admission of guilt as a powerful propaganda tool in the coming war.

Surrender

Washington lost about thirty men during the battle. He marched his remaining troops out of the fort on the morning of July 4,, 1754. The French burned the fort. The battle had disastrous consequences for the British as they now had no outposts of any kind left in the important Ohio River valley with war beckoning.

December 17, 1754 - George Washington Leases Mount Vernon

George Washington signed the lease, granting him lifetime rights to the property from his sister-in-law Anne Washington on December 17, 1754.

Mount Vernon

George Washington's great grandfather, John Washington, and his friend, Nicholas Spencer, acquired the patent for the land that is now Mount Vernon in 1674. He passed the property on to his son, Lawrence, at his death in 1677. Lawrence would divide the 5000-acre property with the heirs of Nicholas Spencer, receiving the smaller of the two portions along Little Hunting Creek. In compensation for receiving the larger share, the Spencer family paid Lawrence 2500 pounds of tobacco, a common medium of exchange during colonial times. George Washington's father, Augustine, acquired the property, first leasing it in 1726. He purchased the property a month after he leased it. Augustine built the first house, a stone structure, on the property. He passed the property on to George's half-brother Lawrence at his death in 1743. Lawrence commenced purchasing more property, primarily from the Spencer tract. He expanded his father's home, calling the estate Mount Vernon in honor of the vice admiral he had served under in the 1740 Cartagena Expedition during the War of Jenkin's Ear.

George Washington Acquires the Property

Lawrence Washington had married Anne Fairfax and would have four children. None of Lawrence's children lived to adulthood. Lawrence died in 1752 of tuberculosis, leaving the property to his only surviving daughter, Sarah. Anne would have a lifetime interest in the property. George had probably been living on the property, managing the plantation. Sarah died in 1754. George leased the property on December 17, 1754. Anne remarried and moved away. At her death in 1761, George inherited the property.

May 10, 1755 - Washington Appointed Aide De Camp to Braddock

After the Council of Royal Governors on April 15, 1755 at Alexandria, Virginia, General Edward Braddock moved quickly to gather a force capable of completing his part in the three-stage plan. The expedition would be the largest ever assembled in the colonies. Braddock meant to expel the French from Fort Duquesne and the Ohio River Valley. Washington had resigned his commission after his capture by the French at Fort Necessity the previous year. The French had noted his bravery in the stand and had paroled Washington and his men. When he learned that Braddock was assembling an army to assault the French and take Fort Duquesne, he applied for a post as a major in the assembling army. However, no colonial could receive an appointment above captain without approval from the London command. Thus, on May 10, 1755, George Washington applied for, and received, a post as a volunteer Aide De Camp to Braddock.

Departure

The British Army had given Braddock the 45th and 48th regiments from Ireland to form the nucleus of his army when he received the title of Commander in Chief of the North American British forces. He managed to add several three companies of American troops. To this, he added an assortment of British artillery, colonial militia and natives, bringing his total force to around 2200 soldiers. On May 29, 1755, Braddock's army departed Fort Cumberland, Maryland for the frontier.

July 9, 1755 - Battle of the Monongahela - French and Indian War

After crossing the Monongahela River a combined French and Indian force engaged British General Edward Braddock in battle. The conflict that ensued cost the British army of almost 1500 soldiers close to a thousand casualties.

Gathering Forces

Braddock established a base at Fort Cumberland, Maryland and proceeded to recruit men. He raised an army of approximately 2200 soldiers. He appointed Colonel George Washington as his aide-de-camp. Washington had led the ill-fated expedition at Fort Necessity, thus he knew the area well. Though plagued by supply and administrative problems he managed to acquire the wagons and horses he needed. This feat occurred through the help of Benjamin Franklin. Finally, on May 29, the expedition departed. Braddock only took around 1400 men and disdained using any Indians to use as guides. Thus, the force only had eight natives in the expedition.

The Trek

Braddock's Expedition moved slowly through the heavily forested terrain. Along the way, they encountered small bands of native warriors along the way. Most of these were allies of the French. They kept the French at Fort Duquesne alerted to their adversaries progress. Braddock divided his force in two. One became a flying column, charged with moving ahead of the main column rapidly. This column did not move rapidly, but moved along slowly through the difficult terrain. By the time the flying column reached the Monongalia River, the French were ready.

Fort Duquesne

The French had kept a small garrison at the fort until the beginning of hostilities. They had reinforced it. But French commander, Claude-Pierre Pecaudy de Contrecoeur, knew it could not stand against Braddock's force. He had about 1600 French, Canadians and native men to defend it. However, the fort's log palisade walls would not stand against the cannon Braddock had with him. Contrecoeur sent Daniel Liénard de Beaujeu out with a French force of about 800 men to ambush the British force as it crossed the river. They arrived too late to ambush them. They ran into a British advance guard under General Thomas Gage. During this fight, the British managed to kill Beaujeu. After the death of Beaujeu, the Canadians fled back to the fort. The Indians continued fighting from behind trees and underbrush. Captain Dumas from Duquesne rallied the Canadians and they rejoined the fight. Braddock's main force now joined Gage's and the battle intensified. Indian tactics frightened the inexperienced British soldiers. The warriors scalped their victims and nailed the scalps on trees for their adversaries to see. This tactic and their terrifying war whoops soon cowed the British force. As the men faltered, Braddock rode through the lines, shouting to and encouraging his men. He had several horses shot out from under him, but he kept rallying the troops until at last they stood firm.

Mortally Wounded

After three hours of intense fighting, Thomas Fausett managed to shoot Braddock through the lung. The fall of Braddock took all the heart out of the British troops and they began a retreat from the field. They managed to carry many of their wounded with them, including the mortally stricken Braddock. They retreated across the river while the Indians plundered the dead they had left behind and imbibing on their rum. The force of 1400 men had lost 456.

July 13, 1755 - General Edward Braddock Dies

Four days after the disastrous Battle of the Monongahela, General Edward Braddock died of the wound he had suffered during the battle.

Mortal Wound

During the latter stages of the July 9, 1755 Battle of the Monongahela, Braddock received a bullet wound through the chest. After he fell, British resistance crumbled and his army fled across the Monongahela River to reorganize. Braddock died on July 13, attended by his aide-de-camp, Colonel George Washington. Before his death, Braddock reportedly bequeathed his ceremonial sash to Colonel Washington, who kept the memento with him the remainder of his life. To prevent the natives from finding the body to desecrate it, his soldiers buried him in the road, at a ceremony presided over by Colonel Washington, and drove wagons over it to hide it. Braddock's Road remained a main road in the years after his death. In 1804 men, doing roadwork discovered human remains and officer's buttons at a spot in the road near the site of Braddock's reported death. Believing the remains to be those of Braddock, locals buried them nearby. Today they rest at Fort Necessity National Battlefield in Pennsylvania.

Fort Necessity National Battlefield

1 Washington Parkway

Farmington, PA 15437

(724) 329-5512

September 17, 1755 - Washington Appointed Colonel Virginia Regiment

During the latter stages of the Battle of the Monongahela, the British troops panicked. Their General Braddock had suffered a serious wound, they had taken heavy casualties and the Indian force that opposed them pressed them hard. Major George Washington, despite suffering a severe fever and headaches, responded to the threat. He rallied the British by riding back and forth across the battlefield, shouting instructions and trying to organize what had become a confused melee. The enemy shot two horses out from under him and after the battle; he had several bullet holes in his coat. However, he succeeded in rallying the troops and conducted an organized retreat. His actions saved what was left of the army.

Appointment as Colonel of the Virginia Regiment

Governor Robert Dinwiddie responded to Braddock's disaster by forming Virginia's first full time military force, the Virginia Regiment. The Regiment initially consisted of 1000 soldiers. Dinwiddie appointed George Washington as Colonel in charge of the Regiment. The governor charged Washington with the defense of the Virginia frontier. A severe disciplinarian, Washington led the regiment into more that twenty battles in ten months. The regiment lost over a third of its recruits. His brutal campaign led to fewer deaths along the Virginia frontier than other colonies had.

July 02, 1758 - Washington Begins Building Road to Fort Duquesne

Brigadier General John Forbes began assembling a force to capture Fort Duquesne in December 1757. In July, Forbes dispatched a force commanded by George Washington to construct a new road to the French fort.

John Forbes (September 5, 1707 – March 11, 1759)

The son of Lieutenant Colonel John Forbes and Elizabeth Graham, John was native to his family estate, Pittencrieff, which is near Dunfermline in Fife, Scotland. His initial desire was to study medicine; however, he changed his mind and entered the military, continuing a family tradition. He enlisted in the Royal Scots Greys, a British cavalry regiment, in 1735. Forbes would see action in War of the Austrian Succession and in the Jacobite rising of 1745. He became a lieutenant colonel of the Royal Scots in 1750 and received command of the 17th Regiment of Foot in 1757. Later in 1757, he received assignment to voyage to North America to fight the French in the Ohio River Valley.

The New Road

Washington wanted to use Braddock's Road that led out from Fort Cumberland in northwestern Maryland. However, the new road would be about thirty-five miles shorter. Washington voiced his complaints several times about the difficulty of building a new road through the densely forested, hilly terrain. But Forbes persisted and on July 2, Washington based his soldiers at Fort Cumberland and began constructing the new road in early August. The new road would include a chain of defensive forts to guard it, the last being Fort Ligionier.

July 24, 1758 - George Washington Elected to Virginia House of Burgesses

George Washington begins his political career with his election to the Virginia House of Burgesses on July 24, 1758. The vote totals for that election are as follows:

Colonel George Washington - 310

Colonel Thomas Bryan Martin - 240

Hugh West - 199

Thomas Swearingen - 45

Total vote - 794

Colonel Washington had been the commander of the local military forces after Braddock's defeat in July 1754. The previous March he had met Mary Custis, a wealthy local widow and had become engaged to her. They would marry in January 1759, a few months after his election.

November 12, 1758 - French Strike British Army near Fort Duquesne

During the twilight hours of November 12, 1758, the French struck Forbes force one last time at the encampment near at Fort Ligonier. Colonel James Burd had assigned a number of soldiers to guard the expedition's horses, which grazed a little over a mile from the fort. A force of about thirty French soldiers and 140 native warriors attacked the widely disbursed soldiers. Forbes ordered George Washington to defend the attack and Colonel Hugh Mercer to take his force and try to flank the enemy. Washington took about 500 soldiers into action. Mercer took an additional 500 men. In the confusion, Mercer's troops accidentally opened fire on Washington's men, killing about thirty-five soldiers and two officers. Washington averted further disaster by riding back and forth in front of Mercer's men striking their muskets with his sword, attempting to get them to stop firing.

The British did manage to capture several French soldiers in the attack. Under interrogation, these soldiers revealed that the natives had abandoned the French at Duquesne and that the fort was in poor condition. The men suffered from poor rations and the garrison much smaller than Forbes initially thought.

November 25, 1758 - George Washington's Troops Occupy Fort Duquesne

The long, arduous expedition led by British General John Forbes finally met success when a contingent of troops led by Colonel George Washington occupied the smoldering remains of Fort Duquesne. Washington, just over five years after the day he first visited the site, became one of the first to visit the fort, destroyed by the French occupiers before escaping into the night on November 24. Washington had desired to receive a commission in the British Army because of his service, but that wish did not materialize. He would resign his commission in the Virginia Regiment soon after the fall of Fort Duquesne.

December 23, 1758 - Washington Resigns Commission - Virginia Regiment

George Washington had begun his military career as a major with his 1753 mission to Fort Le Boeuf. Along the way he had played a role in precipitating the French and Indian War at the May 28, 1754 Battle of Battle of Jumonville Glen and helped end the French threat in the Illinois Country when Fort Duquesne fell on November 25, 1758. With most of his goals reached, Washington resigned his commission in the Virginia Militia as a colonel. He knew his hopes of gaining a commission in the British army were in vain. During his service in the militia, he had seen that British officers disdained their colonial counterparts.

Future at Mount Vernon

Anticipating an end to his military career, Washington had run for election to the Virginia House of Burgesses and won. He would take his seat in February. He had proposed to the widow Martha Custis and she had accepted. Their wedding would take place on January 6, 1759. Almost a year after resigning his commission, Washington and Martha would lease Mount Vernon and make that their home. Washington anticipated that he would spend the remainder of his days as a Virginia planter, legislator and husband. Fate would decree otherwise. The lessons he learned in military tactics, leadership and patience would serve him well almost twenty years later when the colonies entered their epic struggle for independence.

January 6, 1759 - George Washington Marries Martha Dandridge Curtis

Ten months after their first meeting, George Washington married Martha Dandridge Curtis. The wedding occurred on January 6, 1759 at her home, The White House. They had spent less than twenty-four hours in mutual company.

Martha Dandridge Curtis

The first daughter of a Virginia planter, she came into the world on June 2, 1731, near Williamsburg, Virginia. As a girl, she loved riding horses, gardening, sewing, playing the spinet and dancing. Her father, John Dandridge, saw to it that she had a good education in basic mathematics, reading and writing. This was unusual for a girl in the Eighteenth Century. When she turned eighteen, wealthy planter, Daniel Parke Curtis, courted and married her on May 15, 1750. Together they had four children, two of which died in infancy. This was common in a time when only sixty percent of babies survived to adulthood.

The White House

They lived at the White House, an 18th-century plantation on the Pamunkey River in New Kent County, Virginia. The plantation house has not survived the ravages of time. Union General George B. McClellan burned the house on June 28, 1862 as Union Troops retreated during the Seven Days Battles. After the war, ended General W.F. "Rooney" Lee rebuilt the house. It burned down again in 1875. No one ever rebuilt it again.

Widowed

Mr. Curtis died suddenly of an illness in 1757. He left Martha a wealthy widow with two young children. She had 17,000 acres of plantation to run on five plantations and almost 300 hundred slaves to manage. As a widow, her husband's death freed her from coverture. This legal status meant that a husband took over his wife's legal rights and obligations. Mr. Curtis' death meant that now Martha could own property and sign legal papers.

Adjutant General

Virginia created four Adjutant General Offices from Laurence's position after his death. Lieutenant governor Robert Dinwiddie appointed George to one of these four new offices.

Martha and George Meet

It was this position that taught him the art of war, which he found he excelled at during the French and Indian War. He rose in command to "Colonel of the Virginia Regiment and Commander in Chief of all forces now raised in the defense of His Majesty's Colony." He longed for a commission in the British Army, a desire never fulfilled.

He was on leave from his military duties in Williamsburg in 1758 when he heard of Widow Martha Dandridge Curtis. He traveled to her home at The White House where mutual friends introduced them on March 16, 1758.

Engagement and Marriage

Her courtship began, though another Virginia planter, Charles Carter, also paid court to her. They would meet one other time three weeks later and realized that they were meant for each other. George proposed and left for six months to complete his military obligations. During this time, they corresponded by letters, which Martha destroyed the bulk of after his death. He resigned his commission at the end of 1758. He had begun extensive renovations at the plantation house at Mount Vernon. They moved there after their marriage.

The marriage prospered through the tough times of the Revolution and his presidency until his death in 1799. She followed him in death in 1802.

October 15, 1763 - George Washington Surveys Great Dismal Swamp

By 1763, tobacco culture had depleted much of the land along the East Coast, which was becoming scarce. During this period, many Virginia planters and politicians began forming land companies to acquire large quantities of land, wait for the value to rise, and then sell the land at a profit. George Washington and other Virginia planters formed the Dismal Swamp Company to drain a vast area of swampland and develop it into arable land.

Great Dismal Swamp

Located in southeastern Virginia and northeastern North Carolina south of the Chesapeake Bay, the Great Dismal Swamp occupied, by some estimates, over one million acres. William Byrd II, founder of Richmond, Virginia, author and Virginia planter, was one of the first men to explore the area in 1728. He was one of the first men to suggest draining the swamp and many credit him with its name. The swamp became a refuge for escaped slaves, which author Harriet Beecher Stowe wrote about in her novel, Dred: A Tale of the Great Dismal Swamp. In 1974, the United States Congress created the Great Dismal Swamp National Wildlife Refuge. For more information, contact:

Great Dismal Swamp National Wildlife Refuge

3100 Desert Rd

Suffolk, VA 23434

757/986-3705

greatdismalswamp@fws.gov

The Great Dismal Swamp National Wildlife Refuge

https://www.fws.gov/refuge/great_dismal_swamp/

Washington Surveys the Great Dismal Swamp

On October 15, 1763, Washington made the first of many visits to the Great Dismal Swamp. As one of the shareholders of the Dismal Swamp Company, he hoped to profit from draining it and selling the land. Many other wealthy Virginia planters joined in the scheme as well. The shareholders appointed Washington and two other men as managers, responsible for surveying it, securing land titles and executing the plan to drain the swamp. Washington and the others assembled a crew of sixty slaves to dig ditches and make shingles from the cedar trees that grew in the swamp. He visited the swamp several times over the next decade, overseeing the work. The American Revolution diverted Washington from the project.

September 17, 1767 - First Letter George Washington to William Crawford Discussing Land Purchases

The Proclamation of 1763 had banned English settlement west of the Appalachian Mountains. However, Washington's close friend and former French and Indian War compatriot had moved into an area west of this line. Washington was interested in purchasing land in the region in the hopes that he could eventually receive clear title to them. Crawford would visit Washington several times over the next years to discuss the matter and receive money to purchase lands. This association would continue until after the Revolutionary War. The letter Washington sent on September 17 was the second letter that opened this real estate partnership. However, historians have not found the first letter.

May 17, 1769 - George Washington Introduces Anti-Tax Resolutions

In their first political collaboration, Virginia neighbors George Washington, Thomas Jefferson and George Mason introduced a series of political resolutions that called for a boycott of British goods. In a frustrated attempt to stop the legislature, Royal Governor Norborne Berkeley, Baron de Botetourt dissolved the legislature.

Resistance Grows

Resistance to Parliament's passage of the Townsend Duty Acts continued to grow. The British had occupied Boston on October 1, 1768 in a misguided attempt to quell the discontent in the city over the Stamp acts. Parliament had repealed the Stamp Act in 1766, but had passed the Townsend Acts to replace them. The revolutionary group, the Sons of Liberty, had formed an assembly of Massachusetts towns to resist Parliament over the Duty Act. Parliament had declared the assembly illegal and demanded to arrest the protestors and take them back to England for trial.

Townsend Duty Act

The previous Stamp Act had raised many protests in the Colonies and Parliament repealed it. The British Parliament still needed funds to pay the debt incurred by the French and Indian War. The Stamp Act had taxed legal documents, diplomas, almanacs, broadsides, newspapers and playing cards. These things, produced in the Colonies, led to protests that it was an internal tax that Parliament had no right to impose. Parliament repealed this Act. The Townsend Duty Act taxed paint, paper, glass, lead and tea imported into the colonies. Townsend considered this unobjectionable. He felt that these products were externally produced and imported into the colonies.

Widespread Discontent

Parliament believed Colonial resistance consisted of a few firebrands in Boston. However, discontent had been much more widespread among the colonists than the British were aware. Instead of cowing the colonies into compliance, the British occupation of Boston and plan to try protesters in England had inflamed it. Many of the members of the Virginia House of Burgesses had joined to resist the British, including George Mason, George Washington and newly elected Thomas Jefferson.

The Resolutions

George Washington had drawn up the resolutions in April 1769 and sent them to Mason. Mason edited and revised the resolutions and sent them back. Thomas Jefferson had been elected to the House on May 11 and joined their effort. Washington introduced the resolutions on May 17. An enraged Governor Berkeley immediately dissolved the House in an attempt to prevent their passage.

Meeting at Raleigh Tavern

Undeterred, the delegates assembled at Raleigh Tavern and convened there. The resolutions passed despite Berkeley's resistance. Two other colonies, Maryland and South Carolina passed similar resolutions soon after.

December 15, 1769 - George Washington Petitions for Land Promised in 1754

After Washington's return from his mission to Fort Le Boeuf, Dinwiddie had petitioned the Virginia House of Burgesses to raise funds to recruit a militia to repel the French incursions into the Ohio Country. The Burgesses had responded, but due to political issues with Dinwiddie, had not granted enough funds to create the force Dinwiddie needed. In response, Dinwiddie had issued the Proclamation of 1754, granting 200,000 acres of land to the men that joined the militia force. The incentive worked, allowing Washington to recruit his force.

Delays

Washington's actions in the Forks of the Ohio area had precipitated the French and Indian War later in 1754. The successful conclusion of that war by the British in 1763 had tossed the French out of Canada and most of their other North American possessions. The grant of lands promised to Washington and his soldiers met with delays due to King George's Proclamation of 1763, treaties with the natives and other problems.

Petition for the Lands

During the years after the French and Indian Wars, Washington had acquired lands in the Shenandoah Valley and near Williamsburg, Virginia. After he had resigned his commission in the militia, he married Martha Custis. The couple took up residence at Mount Vernon. He thus became a Virginia Planter and, with his election to the Virginia House of Burgesses, a politician. In order to secure his fortune, Washington believed he needed to acquire more land that would increase in value. Thus, now that the requisite treaties with the native tribes had been signed and the land open for settlement, Washington believed the time was right for he and his former comrades to secure the payment they were due. On December 15, 1769, Washington presented a petition to the Virginia House of Burgesses to claim the land promised by Dinwiddie's Proclamation of 1754.

Approval

The House approved Washington's request, on condition that he have the land surveyed before taking possession of the land. The land in question would consist of twenty tracts of land along the Great Kanawha and Ohio Rivers. In

October 1770, Washington would depart on an expedition to help survey these tracts.

July 05, 1774 - Washington and Others Meet at Alexandria, Virginia

George Washington, Charles Broadwater George Mason, Patrick Henry and other representatives from Fairfax County met at Alexandria to form a committee that would write a statement defining the colonist's constitutional rights. They would also draft a set of instructions to give to the delegates that would attend Virginia's special convention in August. The Fairfax Resolves, approved later in July, were the result of this effort.

July 17, 1774 - George Mason, Patrick Henry and George Washington Write Fairfax Resolves

Meeting in Fairfax County, Virginia at Washington's plantation, Mount Vernon, George Mason, Patrick Henry and George Washington wrote a document that historians have come to call the Fairfax Resolves. The document, revolutionary in concept, outlined what the authors believed was their natural, constitutional rights and called for a colonial association to meet to deal with their disputes with Britain. The rights outlined in the document included controls over:

Taxation

Parliamentary Representation

Judicial Powers

Control over Military Forces within their Borders

Commerce

July 18, 1774 - Virginia Convention Passes Fairfax Resolves

The day after writing the document, George Washington took the document to Alexandria, Virginia to submit to the delegates of the Virginia Convention. After making some minor changes, the delegates passed the resolution.

June 15, 1775 - John Adams Nominates George Washington Commander in Chief

On June 15, 1775, John Adams nominated Virginian George Washington to serve as the commander in chief of the newly created Continental Army. Washington had proven himself as a competent military leader in the French and Indian War, which had ended twelve years prior. He had also acquired a favorable "national" reputation among the other colonies. Adams hoped that Washington would prove a unifying force for the colonies.

June 19, 1775 - Continental Congress Commissions George Washington as Commander in Chief

On June 19, 1775 members of the Continental Congress voted, by unanimous vote, to appoint George Washington as commander in chief of the Continental Army.

Differing Opinions

Most of the militiamen that had gathered around Boston were New Englanders, leading many of the New England delegates to believe that a New Englander should serve as commander in chief. Others believed that they needed to appoint an outsider to build support from the other colonies and make it a true Continental Army.

Ideal Choice

George Washington's extensive military experience during the French and Indian War made him on of the few delegates at the Continental Congress with wartime experience. Politically, he was a moderate that, at the beginning of the Congress, hoped the colonies could avoid war. However, like the majority of other delegates, he feared that war was unavoidable. Washington was also from Virginia and as one of the larger colonies, it was important to include someone from it. He had arrived in Philadelphia on May 10. Before his arrival at the Congress, he had an indentured servant named Andrew Judge make a uniform of Washington's design. It was blue and buff and was meant to instill confidence in his fellow delegates at the Congress. He wore this uniform throughout his stay in Philadelphia.

Misgivings

After his appointment, Washington expressed misgivings to his wife, Martha, who would now be alone at Mount Vernon. However, he felt it was his duty to accept. Washington accepted the commission and made plans to depart for Boston to take command of an impromptu army.

June 23, 1775 - Washington Departs Philadelphia for Massachusetts

After a review of the militia troops in Philadelphia, General George Washington and his entourage departed Philadelphia for Cambridge, Massachusetts where Washington would take command of the troops.

The Entourage

Major General Charles Lee, his aide Samuel Griffin, Major General Philip Schuyler, his military secretary Joseph Reed and Washington's aide de camp Thomas Mifflin accompanied General Washington on the trip. Charles Lee was technically third in command of the Continental Army, behind Washington and Artemas Ward. Major General Philip Schuyler would take command of the Northern Division at New York when the group reached that city.

The Route

The officers departed Philadelphia, traveling up the Delaware River to Trenton. From Trenton, the entourage would travel through New Brunswick, Newark and Hoboken, New Jersey before arriving in New York on June 25.

June 25, 1775 - General Washington Arrives New York

When General Washington reached New York, a large crowd of enthusiastic New Yorkers met him shouting huzzahs. After his arrival, he wrote three letters. The first was to give instructions to General Philip Schuyler, who would take command of the Northern Department of the Continental Army. The second letter was to John Hancock, who was serving as the president of the Massachusetts Provincial Congress. In the letter he discussed the June 17 Battle of Bunker Hill and that he had discovered 1000 pounds of gunpowder in the city. Washington had sent the gunpowder on to Cambridge. The shipment had left no gunpowder in New York City. In the third letter to the Continental Congress, he stressed the point that gunpowder was in short supply.

July 03, 1775 - George Washington Takes Command of the Continental Army

George Washington had arrived in Cambridge, Massachusetts on July 2, 1775. Tradition states that on July 3, 1775 Washington took command of the army under an elm tree on the town common during a military ceremony. Many historians believe that Ward transferred command to Washington in the Wadsworth House, then owned by Harvard President Samuel Langdon. Washington established his headquarters in the John Vassall, Jr. home, a Tory who had fled to Boston.

Washington's Staff

The Continental Congress had appointed a number of officers to serve on Washington's staff as he strove to create an army out of the disorganized mass of men that had surrounded Boston. These men were:

Major General Artemas Ward - Senior Officer

Major General Charles Lee

Major General Philip Schuyler

Major General Israel Putnam

Numerous other brigadier generals also served in various capacities.

The Army

Washington, after reviewing the troops, observed that this army was composed of "a mixed multitude of people under very little discipline, order or government." Artemas Ward, who had been in command, estimated the numbers of soldiers that made up to be around 18,000 - 20,000 men. Washington later determined the number to be more in the neighborhood of 14,000 soldiers. This "army" was not under any central command. It was a loosely organized band of militia forces under the command of the various states from which they originated. No coordinated system of feeding or providing supplies existed. The soldiers had little or no training and largely came and went, as they desired. Somehow, out of this disorganized rabble of men Washington and his staff had to create an army that could stand up to the best army in the world, the British Army.

October 19, 1781 - General George Washington Defeats General Cornwallis at Yorktown Virginia

After two weeks of American and French bombardment, siege and attacks, Lieutenant General Charles Cornwallis signaled to the allied French and Americans that he was ready to negotiate terms of surrender. Negotiations began the next day.

The British Surrender

On the morning of October 19, 1781, British troops emerged from Yorktown with flags furled and shouldered muskets. The soldiers laid their muskets down between the watching American and French allies. General Cornwallis, citing illness, did not attend the elaborate ceremony in which about 8,000 British and Hessian troops surrendered.

The Battle of Yorktown had ended in a stunning American and French victory, which ended all major fighting in the North American colonies.

The war was over, though the official peace treaty would not be signed for almost two years.

July 26, 1788 - First Use of the Official Northwest Territory Seal

The first known use of the Seal of the Northwest Territory was on a proclamation that Governor Arthur St. Clair issued on July 26, 1788. The seal includes a coiled snake, a felled tree, boats on the river and a heavily laden apple tree.

A Latin inscription reads, with the translation below:

"*Meliorem lapsa locavit!*'

"He has planted a better than the fallen."

The outer inscription on the seal is:

"The Seal of The Territory Of The US Northwest Of The River Ohio"

December 15, 1788 - First Election Northwest Territory

The Northwest Territory Act of 1787 decreed that when the territory's population grew to 5,000 free males of full age, the inhabitants became entitled to hold election. The first election in the Northwest Territory occurred on third Monday in December, December 15, 1798. The voters chose twenty-two representatives for the Territorial general assembly. These representatives met at the territorial capital of Cincinnati to choose ten names as candidates for the upper house. President John Adams chose five men from this list to serve in the chamber's upper house. These men used laws from existing states, mostly Pennsylvania, as guidance.

December 28, 1788 - Losantiville (Cincinnati) Established

Cincinnati plays a role in the settlement of Indiana as the land office in Cincinnati sold some of the first tracts of land in the future state.

George Rogers Clark built temporary fortifications on the site in 1780 as part of his extensive operations against Indian tribes fighting for the British in the Revolutionary War. Revolutionary War soldiers received land grants as part of their pay for service, and John Cleves Symmes had received a grant that included this plot of land after the war. On December 28, 1788, a group of settlers led by Colonel Robert Patterson arrived at the 740 acres site and began laying out a settlement. These settlers named the new city Losantiville. This name was an anagram formed from the French and Latin words for "city opposite the mouth of the Licking River.

1788 - Francis Godfrey Born

Francis Godfroy (1788–1840)

Palaanswa, his Miami name, was the son of a Miami woman and a French fur trader. Palaanswa was the Miami interpretation of his given name, François. After the Americans stepped up attacks on the Miami tribe, Chief Godfrey became one of the leaders of Miami resistance. He led the Miami attack at the Battle of the Mississinewa in 1812. He turned trader after the war, establishing a trading post at the junction of the Mississinewa and Wabash Rivers. Serving as the broker between the natives and the Americans, he managed the sale of several land deals. He managed to slow the cession of land while gaining higher payments for the tribes than many of the other tribes. He also obtained exemptions from many of the Miami for their removal from the state. He and these that stayed behind are the foundation of the Miami Nation of Indiana. He also acquired a large quantity of land that served as a refuge for many of the Miami when they later returned to Indiana.

The Indiana Historical Bureau has installed an historical marker in Montpelier, Indiana:

Title of Marker:

Godfroy Reserve

Location:

SE corner of Main Street & Huntington Street/SR 18, Montpelier. (Blackford County, Indiana)

Installed by:

Erected by Francois Godfroy Chapter NSDAR 1989

Marker ID #:

05.1989.1

Marker Text:

Reserved by U.S. to Chief Francois Godfroy of the Miami Nation of Indians by treaty at St. Mary's, Ohio, 6 October 1818, 3, 840 acres on Salamonie River at La Petite Prairie, Harrison Township, Blackford County; reserve lands sold 1827, 1836.

1788 - Vincennes Donation Lands

During the years before the American Revolution, the French had not been careful record keepers in regards to their land grants. This led to much confusion after American settlement began. To bring order to the confusion the act authorizing the donations provided for the French lands to be surveyed and recorded. The grant included 400 acres of land with 160 separate plots. Later, Congress made additional grants in another five counties. The Indiana Historical Bureau has installed an historical marker in Washington, Indiana.

Title of Marker:

Vincennes Donation Lands

Location:

Intersection of US 50 bypass & SR 57, grassy median between restaurant & motel (as of 12/2003), 7 Cumberland Drive, Washington. (Daviess County, Indiana)

Installed by:

Erected by Indiana Sesquicentennial Commission, 1966

Marker ID #:

14.1966.1

Marker Text:

In 1788 Congress granted 400 acres of land to each French family of this area. The tract was laid off in a square containing 160 separate plots. Additional grants were made affecting the five counties shown.

Events of 1789

January 09, 1789 - Treaty of Fort Harmar

Governor Arthur St. Clair appealed to the various native tribes to sign a treaty to end the bloodshed along the frontier. On December 13, 1788, representatives from the Wyandot, Delaware, Ottawa, Chippewa, Pottawatomie, and the Sauk nations gathered at the fort to begin negotiations. The Indians demanded that St. Clair reserve the area west of the Muskingum River and north of the Ohio River for them. St. Clair would not agree to that and in turn demanded that the tribes adhere to the boundaries agreed to at the 1785 Treaty of Fort Mackintosh. The tribes would not agree to this, so St. Clair threatened them that he would attack them. At length he gave them $3,000 in gifts if they would sign. The treaty signing took place on January 9. Because they had not attended the meeting, the Shawnee, Miami, Kickapoo and other tribes along the Wabash River did not recognize the treaty.

February 02, 1789 - John Cleves Symmes Arrives North Bend

Judge John Cleves Symmes and sixty settlers arrived at the mouth of the Miami River to found North Bend near the Losantiville settlement.

John Cleves Symmes (July 21, 1742 – February 26, 1814)

The son of Timothy and Mary Cleves Symmes, John was native to Riverhead, New York. Symmes studied law and gained his law license, after which he married Anna Tuthill. The couple would have three children. The youngest daugher, Anna Tuthill Symmes, married future Indiana Territorial Governor William Henry Harrison. Symmes served as chairman of the New Jersey Sussex County Committee of Safety in 1774.

Revolutionary War

He enlisted in the 3rd Regiment of the Sussex County militia as a colonel when the Revolutionary War began and later gained election to the New Jersey Legislative Council in 1776.

Politics and Land Speculator

From 1785 through 1786, he served in the Confederation Congress. He also served as a member of the New Jersey Supreme Court. In 1788, Symmes purchased 311,682 acres along the Ohio River. President George Washington signed the land patent on October 30, 1794. Known as the Symmes Purchase, the judge published a pamphlet on November 26, 1787, entitled *To the Respectable Public*. The pamphlet advertised the sale of the lands, which sold quickly.

Settler

Symmes decided he wanted to settle on these lands, so he gathered sixty pioneers and sailed down the Ohio River, landing at the site on February 2, 1789. Symmes had the town of North Bend platted into forty-eight lots. Symmes and his other investors chose not to utilize the surveying system devised by the United States Government, instead using one of his own systems. This created scores of land title problems for those that purchased land from him. This resulted several changes in land survey laws later on.

Maxwell's Code

Symmes was instrumental in the development of Maxwell's Code. He also developed an adversarial relationship with Territorial Governor Arthur St. Clair. Symmes passed away on February 26, 1814 and interred in Congress Green Cemetery in North Bend, Ohio.

February 04, 1789 - George Washington Elected President

On February 4, 1789, members of the Electoral College met in their respective state capitals and cast their ballots for the President of the United States. George Washington received sixty-nine Electoral Votes. Only ten of the original thirteen states selected electors for this first election as Rhode Island and North Carolina had not yet ratified the Constitution. New York, in the middle of a legislative conflict, did not choose electors in time for the election.

In the system in place in 1788, the electors actually cast two separate ballots. The first ballot was for President, of which Washington was the unanimous winner with sixty-nine votes. The second ballot was for Vice President with John Adams winning this with thirty-four votes, with ten other men receiving votes.

Others receiving votes for President in the Electoral College were:

John Jay (9)

Robert H. Harrison (6)

John Rutledge (6)

John Hancock (4)

George Clinton (3)

Samuel Huntington (2)

John Milton (2)

James Armstrong (1)

Benjamin Lincoln (1)

Edward Telfair (1)

February 06, 1789 - First Marriage in Newly Organized Northwest Territory

On February 6, 1789, Winthrop Sargent and Rowena Tupper, with Rufus Putnam officiating, married in Marietta, becoming the first official wedding recorded in the Northwest Territory.

Winthrop Sargent (May 1, 1753 – June 3, 1820)

The son of Winthrop and Judith Saunders Sargent, Winthrop was native to Gloucester, Massachusetts. Sargent attended Harvard College, after which he captained one of his father's merchant ships until the American Revolution broke out. On July 7, 1775, he enlisted as a lieutenant in the Continental Army. He participated in several campaigns, including Trenton, Brandywine, Germantown, and Monmouth, rising steadily in command to captain. He attained the rank of brevet major before mustering out August 25, 1783. He helped survey the Seven Ranges in eastern Ohio, which was the first land surveyed using the Public Land Survey system in 1786. Congress appointed him as the first Secretary in the Northwest Territory, a post he started in 1788 in Marietta.

Rowena Tupper Sargent (1766 - 1790)

The daughter of Benjamin and Huldah White Tupper, Rowena was probably native to Chesterfield, Massachusetts. She and Winthrop Sargent married, however Rowena died in childbirth about a year later. The child also died.

July 27, 1789 - John Cleve Moves to Crawford's Ford

The Cleve family had settled initially on his friend Robert Benham's farm on the North Fork of Ten Mile Creek after their arrival in December 1785. When spring arrived, Cleve built a small log cabin on a tract of land where he farmed and worked as a blacksmith. In 1788, John moved his family closer to Washington, Pennsylvania. The main occupants of the town at the time were German immigrants. Hardworking and pious, Cleve found them a friendly lot. The other main group of people living there were poor Irish tenant farmers. The next year Cleve began preparing to move his family to John Symmes' new settlement at Losantiville. On July 27, 1789, his daughter Amy entered the world and he moved the family to Crawford's Ford on the Monongahela River. Here, he set up a blacksmith shop and began building a flatboat to move his family down the Monongahela River to the Ohio and on into the Northwest Territory.

Flatboats

The flatboat was the primary means settlers along river and large streams used to transport goods and their possessions downriver to settle downriver. A flatboat was a rectangular, flat-bottomed boat used to transport both settlers, their families, their possessions or freight. A farmer unskilled in boat building could build a flat boat and fill it with his family and possessions. Usually, at voyage end, the settler disassembled the flatboat and sold the lumber, or used it for construction.

August 09, 1789 - Army Troops Arrive at North Bend to Construct Fort Washington

Captain David Strong arrived on August 11 followed by Major John Doughty on August 11 to construct a fort to protect Losantiville and North Bend in what is now southwestern Ohio.

David Strong (July 6, 1744 - August 19, 1801)

The son of Josiah Strong and Elizabeth Strong, David was native to Litchfield, Connecticut. He enlisted in the Continental Army as a sergeant. The British captured his unit during the Battle of the Cedars near Quebec in May

1776. Strong mustered out after the war, but reenlisted later on. He married Chloe Richmond with whom he would have five children. During the decade of the 1790, he helped supervise the building of many of the forts in the Ohio Valley region. In 1800 Strong, who had been promoted to colonel, took nineteen flatboats with 400 troops from Pittsburg to a point between the Tennessee and Mississippi Rivers to build a fort. The new fort would be sixteen miles downriver of Fort Massac. The men cleared 400 acres and began construction of the fort in the spring of 1801. Strong served as the commander of Fort Wilkinson, in Wilkinsonville, Illinois, where he died of injuries suffered during a tornado. Strong's wife and son were with him at the new fort and returned to Cincinnati after his death.

John Doughty (July 25, 1754 – September 16, 1826)

Native to New York City, Doughty enlisted in the Continental Army on January 13, 1776. Doughty's service included appointments as adjutant general of two battalions and captain lieutenant of the New Jersey Eastern Artillery Company. He fought at several battles, including Brandywine (1777), Germantown (1777), Monmouth (1778), Springfield (1780), and Yorktown (1781). After the war, he commanded a detachment of twenty-five men that guarded leftover supplies from the war at Fort Pitt. Brigadier General Josiah Harmar promoted Doughty to major and put him in charge of constructing Fort Harmar and later Fort Washington. Doughty retired from the army in 1800 and lived at his private estate in New Jersey, where he died in 1826. Doughty married Margaret Maring, with whom he would have one child, a daughter. He is interred at First Presbyterian Church Cemetery in Morristown.

Fort Washington

Before construction of the fort, the settlements on the north bank of the river had only two blockhouses, one of which

George Rogers Clark had constructed in 1780, and a small fort constructed by John Cleves Symmes. Major Doughty spent several days inspecting various sites for the fort and finally chose a spot opposite the Licking River in Kentucky about 500 feet from the river between Third and Broadway Streets in current Cincinnati. Doughty designed the fort, however construction was supervised by Lieutenant John Pratt, and newly arrived Captain William Ferguson. The fort was of typical design for Ohio River Valley forts, square with two story blockhouses at each corner. The second story of the blockhouse projected out over the palisade that connected the blockhouses and allowed defenders to lay down a defensive fire against any attackers that approached the walls. The troops cleared the ground for the fort and for a considerable distance around it. The trees they cut served as construction materials. They cut twenty-foot logs and placed the ends in four-foot deep trenches. The resulting palisade, with the log's tips sharpened, presented a formidable barrier to any attacker. The soldiers tore flatboats that brought supplies downriver apart and used the lumber for doors, roofs and floor in the fort. The flatboats were made for a one-way trip downriver and the Army could buy them cheaply for use in the fort. The completed fort could hold a garrison of 1500 troops. General Harmar took command of the new Fort Washington on December 29, 1789.

Events of 1790

January 02, 1790 - Hamilton County Established - Ohio

Northwest Territorial Governor Arthur St. Clair issued a proclamation on January 2, 1790 that created the second county formed in the Territory. St. Clair allowed John Cleves Symmes, who had originally purchased the tract of land, the honor of naming the new county. Symmes chose to name it in honor of Alexander Hamilton, the current Treasurer of the United States.

Alexander Hamilton (January 11, 1755 or 1757 – July 12, 1804)

The son of James A. Hamilton and Rachel Faucette, Alexander was native to Charlestown, Nevis, which is southeast of Puerto Rico. Historians are not sure of the exact year Hamilton was born, and Hamilton was not even sure. January 11, 1755 is the most accepted date. Alexander's mother had married, under pressure from her family, a Danish merchant named John Lavien when she was quite young. Lavien was much older than Rachel was and subjected her to abuse. He also spent the greater part of her inheritance and had accused her of adultery, for which he had her imprisoned. When the authorities released her, she left Lavien and their son and traveled to St. Kitts Island. She met James Hamilton and the two moved in together. Her husband found out about their relationship and divorced her. Danish law forbade her from remarrying, so Alexander and his older brother, also born of the union, were considered illegitimate.

Orphaned and Finance Prodigy

Rachel died when Alexander was about ten. His father, James, had abandoned Alexander and his older brother about three years previously. A cousin took him in. Knowledge of his early life is sketchy. He appears to be largely self-educated. His family sent him to an export-import firm to work when he was eleven years old. There, Hamilton learned early the mechanics of international finance. Impressed by the boy's intelligence, a Presbyterian minister named Hugh Knox and Alexander's boss, Nicolas Cruger, raised money to send Hamilton to New York to attend King's University (now Columbia). Knox had become impressed with Alexander when he read a letter the boy wrote about a hurricane he witnessed in 1772. Thus, when he was about sixteen years old, Hamilton arrived in New York in 1773, on the eave of the Revolutionary War.

College

Hamilton attended King's College, now Columbia University, in 1773, until the British forced its closing when they occupied New York in 1776. He continued education on his own until he gained his law license in 1782.

Militia

Hamilton joined a militia unit called the Corsicans, later renamed the Hearts of Oak, sometime between April and June 1775. In 1776, he raised a company of artillery called the New York Provincial Company of Artillery, to which he gained election as captain. During the war, he participated in the Battle of Princeton. In 1777, General George Washington asked him to serve as his chief of staff, a role he accepted and performed for the next four years. He received command of the 1st and 2d New York Regiments near war's end and played a role in the Continental Army's victory over the British at Yorktown.

Politician

After the war, New York appointed him as a representative in the Congress of the Confederation in July 1782 for a short stint. He gained his law degree during this period, resigned from the Congress and returned to New York to found the

Bank of New York. He gained election to the New York State Legislature in 1787 and received appointment to serve in the Constitutional Convention. He, along with John Jay and James Madison, played an essential role in the Constitution's ratification by writing The Federalist Papers. George Washington invited Hamilton to serve in his administration as the first Secretary of the Treasury.

January 03, 1790 - John Van Cleve and his Family Settle Losantiville

The Van Cleve family boarded the flatboat John had built on December 25, 1789. The voyage downstream proved uneventful. They kept a constant watch on the north shore for signs of Indian activity; however, they saw none. No canoes or any other vessel appeared on the entire voyage. They left the flatboat drift both day and night, making good time. They passed the Scioto River's mouth on January 1, 1790 and landed at Losantiville on January 3. At this time, only two hewed log houses and a few cabins stood on the site and construction of Fort Washington had just been completed. The Van Cleve family settled on land owned by Major David Leitch. Leitch, who had migrated into the area in 1789, had offered anyone that would clear ten acres of land for him 100 acres. Van Cleve cleared the required acreage for Leitch and received his grant of 100 acres.

January 04, 1790 - St. Clair Renames Lonsantiville to Cincinnati

General Arthur St. Clair arrived at Fort Washing on January 2, 1790 for a short visit. During his short stay, he approved of Harmar's choice of Fort Washington, honoring General George Washington. However, he took issue with the settlement of Losantiville. Not liking the name, he decided to honor the society of Revolutionary War soldiers to which he belonged, the Society of the Cincinnati.

Unfolding Strategy

Fort Washington complemented a long line of forts planned along the Ohio River meant to allow troops to penetrate deep into the interior of the Northwest Territory to attack the native villages. His headquarters at Marietta had been the center of this line of forts when he located there two years before. It was too far east now, as the line of forts now extended west to Fort Steuban at the Falls of the Ohio. The Americans had plans for more forts extending in a line west from Fort Steuban to the Mississippi River. St. Clair envisioned two more lines of forts, one along the Maumee River in the north and another along the Wabash River in the west. Fort Washington, the largest and most powerful of the new forts, and Cincinnati would be the capital of this new, developing empire. St. Clair would make Fort Washington his capital later that year.

Society of the Cincinnati

Officers that served in the Continental Army during he Revolutionary War established the Society of the Cincinnati in May 1783 in Newburgh, New York. The name derives from a Roman general, Lucius Quinctius Cincinnatus. Membership in the organization is hereditary, open only to heirs of the founders. This has since been changed to allow descendents of officers that served in the Revolution, even if they had not joined the Society when it began. George Washington served as the first president of the Society. Society of the Cincinnati

2118 Massachusetts Avenue, NW,

Washington, DC 20008

202.785.2040

https://www.societyofthecincinnati.org/

Lucius Quinctius Cincinnatus (c.519 – c.430 BC)

Cincinnatus has come to embody the traits of civic virtue and manliness because of his selfless service to the Roman republic during a time of crises. Cincinnatus worked a small farm near Rome. A hostile army of the Aequi tribe, native to the Italian peninsula and a fierce opponent of Rome, had surrounded a Roman army at the crest of Mount Algidus southeast of Rome. The Romans appointed Cincinnatus absolute ruler and general of the Roman army. According to legend, Cincinnatus left his farm and defeated the Aequi in one day. After saving the Republic, Cincinnatus ceded power and returned to his farm. Although he is an historical figure, the story of Cincinnatus had acquired many legendary accounts.

January 23, 1790 - Governor Arthur St. Clair Sends Message to Major John Hamtramck

While at Fort Steuban St. Clair sent dispatches to Vincennes commander Major Jean François Hamtramck. These dispatches contained messages of peace to the Wabash Indian tribes. He also addressed a shortage of corn in Vincennes, relating that there was plenty of corn in Clarksville if the people of Vincennes could pay for it.

From Fort Steuban, the Governor departed for Kaskaskia, Illinois on the Mississippi River to organize the government there.

From Clarksville, the Governor departed for Kaskaskia, Illinois on the Mississippi River to organize the government there.

March 09, 1790 - Israel Ludlow Establishes Ludlow's Station

Israel Ludlow established Ludlow's Station near Mill Creek about five miles north of the Ohio River on March 9, 1790. The location of his settlement and accompanying blockhouse was at the approximate location of Mad Anthony and Knowlton Streets in Cincinnati. An historical marker and memorial park denote the approximate location.

Israel Ludlow (1765 - January 20, 1804)

The son of Colonel Cornelius and Martha Lyon Ludlow, Israel was native to Long Hill, New Jersey. Ludlow received training as a surveyor and gained appointment as a surveyor working for Thomas Hutchins, Surveyor General of the United States sometime before 1787. Hutchins appointed him to survey the still uncompleted South Carolina portion of the Seven Ranges. Later that same year he surveyed a one million acre tract for the Ohio Company of Associates along the Ohio River, a tract now known as Israel Ludlow's Survey. John Cleves Symmes hired Ludlow to establish the boundaries of his tract in 1788. Matthias Denman, Robert Patterson, and John Filson had agreed to establish the settlement they would call Losantiville on August 25, 1788. However, Filson died and Ludlow replaced him. Ludlow completed the survey of the town in 1789. Governor St. Clair appointed Ludlow as clerk of Hamilton County when he established it on January 2, 1790. Three months later, Ludlow established Ludlow Station. He and the other settlers of the new settlement built a blockhouse at the site.

Stations

Many of the new settlers established stations, which consisted of a blockhouse and possibly a few cabins surrounding it. Many times the new residents lived in the blockhouses with any families that accompanied them. The blockhouse provided protection from Indian attack.

March 16, 1790 - Hamtramck Dispatches Peace Message Up the Wabash

In a final attempt to secure peace between the Wabash River tribes and the American settlers, Major Jean François Hamtramck dispatched a messenger bearing an offer of peace from his commander, General Arthur St. Clair.

Increased Settlement

The Ohio River Valley became the target of increased settlement during the years after the Revolutionary War ended. Flatboats containing new settlers, their livestock and tools voyaged down the river as Americans searched for new land in the region ceded by Great Britain at the end of the war. The winter of 1787 – 1788 saw almost 3000 new settlers carried by over 170 flatboats down the river.

Time of Conflict

In the years, leading up to 1790 both American settlers and natives had conducted raids against each other. The British exacerbated the situation by maintaining military bases across the region around the Great Lakes as they attempted to build an Indian nation between Canada and the United States. Each raid precipitated a retaliatory strike. Major Hamtramck, commandant of Vincennes, could do little to stop the conflict. He had attempted several times to generate a peace agreement with the tribes, but failed. General Arthur St. Clair, now ensconced in his new headquarters at Fort Washington on the Ohio, authorized Major Hamtramck to make one last try. Thus, on March 16, 1790, Hamtramck dispatched Pierre Gamelin to travel up the Wabash to the Miami tribes to make another attempt.

Failed Attempt

Pierre traveled upriver to the tribes that inhabited villages at the mouth of the Vermillion River, near present day Cayuga,

Indiana. Here, the natives would allow him to travel no further up the Wabash. Pierre retuned to Vincennes, the attempt having failed. St. Clair would make one further attempt in April.

April 05, 1790 - Antoine Gamelin Sent to Ouiatenon

Major John Hamtramck received the message from Governor Arthur St. Clair to send a peace delegation to Fort Ouiatenon sometime in February or March. He sent Pierre Gamelin up the Wabash on to make an appeal to the tribes, however, Pierre's mission failed. On April 5, Hamtramck sent Pierre's brother, Antoine, a French fur trader that was visiting Vincennes, on one last attempt.

Early History

The Eastern Iroquois had driven many of the original inhabitants out of this region along the Wabash River, a few miles south of Lafayette, early in the Seventeenth Century. By the late 1600's, these tribes began returning to the area. It was an ideal site for settlement, as the deepwater region of the Wabash begins nearby. The Wea Creek emptied into the Wabash, providing and ideal feeding area for fish. The surrounding plains contained an abundance of wildlife. The natives could grow their crops in the fertile, loamy prairie soil. These natives, a Miami speaking tribe, came to be known as the Wea, forming a number of villages grew up in the area.

Fort Ouiatenon

The French, in their bid to control North America, built Fort Ouiatenon in 1717, making it the first European structure in what would become the State of Indiana. They named it Ouiatenon, a Wea word meaning "place of the whirlpool." The French encouraged the growth of the fort as a trading post for the local tribes. It soon became one of the more important trading posts in the region, perhaps having as many as 2000 - 3000 inhabitants. Its location, about eighteen miles below the mouth of the Tippecanoe River and about five miles south of the current city of Lafayette, was opposite a large Wea village on the banks of the Wabash River. French fur traders descended the Wabash River once a year to trade goods that the natives needed for the furs they had gathered. Many of these traders remained in the village, often described as the finest trading post in the upper country. The village inside the stockade consisted of a double row of ten houses, chapel, blacksmith shop and trading places. Outside the walls almost ninety houses stood. During the approximately forty-year period of French occupation, the French and the natives coexisted in relative peace.

This portion of the article excerpted from the author's book:

Exploring Indiana's Historic Sites, Markers & Museums North West Edition

http://mossyfeetbooks.blogspot.com/2016/06/exploring-indianas-historic-sites_10.html

The French and Indian War (1754 - 1763) ended this tranquil period. The French, as per terms of the Treaty of Paris, abandoned the fort when they departed North America at the wars conclusion. The British occupied the fort after the French departed, but did not develop the same close relationship with the natives that the French had. The native tribes did not like the British policies towards them. An Ottawa chief named Pontiac led an uprising against British forces. His plan included having native forces capture several British forts simultaneously. Pontiac's plan to drive the British out of North America received an additional boost when a band of Wea, Kickapoo and Mascouten captured Fort Ouiatenon without firing a shot, on June 1, 1763. The British abandoned the fort after the war ended.

Revolutionary War

During the Revolutionary War, Captain Leonard Helm, part of George Roger's Clark's force that captured Vincennes, visited the area long enough to acquire loyalty pledges from the local French and natives that occupied the area. British Lieutenant Governor Henry Hamilton paused during his downriver foray to recapture Vincennes in 1778. During his short sojourn, he reprimanded the occupants for allying themselves with the Americans. After making further preparations to retake Vincennes, he departed.

British Interference

After the Revolution, the Ouiatenon area remained peaceful. The growing influx of white settlers enraged the local tribes and they began using the fort built by the French as a staging area to attack American settlements in the east. The British received substantial income from fur trade with the native tribes in the Northwest Territory and wanted it to continue. Thus, the British Governor of Canada, Sir Guy Carleton, encouraged the raids against American settlers and supplied them with arms and supplies. The Northwest Territory's population in early 1791 was around 4280 whites. From 1784 until 1791, the natives killed about 1500 settlers.

Antoine Gamelin (June 15, 1767 - May 14, 1819)

Brother of Pierre Gamelin and the son of Pierre Gamelin and Joseph LaJeunesse, Antoine was native to Longueuil, Quebec, Canada. The Gamelin brothers traded extensively with the Indians along the Wabash River and knew the chiefs personally. Antoine agreed to take St. Clair's speeches to the natives along the Wabash. Gamelin would marry Marie Madeline Foucreau in 1802, with whom he would have one son. He drowned in the St. Lawrence River near LaPrairie, Quebec, Canada in 1819.

The Message

St. Clair's message to the chiefs of the Wabash included a plea for peace with the tribes in the Northwest Territory. The letters consisted of a speech to them from St. Clair proposing a peach conference between the Miami and Kickapoo to be held at Vincennes.

April 07, 1790 - General Josiah Harmar Report on Shawnee Attacks on the Ohio River

General James Wilkinson filed a report to Secretary of War Henry Knox relating several attacks along the Ohio River that threatened to end navigation along that vital watercourse.

Danger on the River

By spring of 1790, navigation along the Ohio River had become a dangerous endeavor. Almost daily Shawnee and warriors from other tribes attacked settlers floating down the river on flatboats, killing many and destroying much property. A band of Shawnee had encamped near the mouth of the river and staged raids on flatboats as they voyaged downriver to settlements in northern Kentucky and the Northwest Territory. One ploy the natives used was to display a white captive near the shore in an attempt to lure those in the boats to venture ashore to rescue them. When the would-be rescuers neared the shore, or landed, the warriors fell upon them, killing or capturing them. Usually they would then throw those killed back into the boat to allow them to float downstream for horrified settlers to find. Sometime in late March or early April this band of natives had attacked a convoy of five flatboats about fifteen miles above the settlement of Limestone (now called Maysville),

Kentucky. The warriors killed everyone in the flatboats and set them adrift. Harmar planned to stage a retaliatory strike against the marauders in mid April.

April 09, 1790 - Gamelin Reaches the Village of the Piankeshaw

By April 9, 1790, Antoine Gamelin and his party had reached the region of the Vermillion River, a distance of about 105 river miles and about fifteen miles north of the current town of Montezuma. Gamelin encountered two villages of the Piankeshaw tribe here, the first one a village called Kikaponguoi. At Kikaponguoi, the chief received him well and took the speeches given him by Gamelin. The chief of the Piankeshaw at this village also gave him a good reception; however, he would not give Gamelin an answer to the speeches until he knew the disposition of the tribes inhabiting the Miami Town (Kekionga). The chief requested that he continue on to Kekionga and then report to him what kind of reception the Shawnee living there gave him. With that, Gamelin continued on his journey upriver.

Piankeshaw

The Piankeshaw lived in scattered villages in west and southwestern Indiana. They inhabited villages along the White River with their main village near Vincennes. As white settlement increased and tension between the natives and the Americans increased, they moved away from Vincennes. The tribe split, with one branch moving to the region around Kaskaskia and the other to inhabit the lands around the Vermillion River in west central Indiana about thirty miles north of Terra Haute. Closely allied with the Miami Tribe, they lived separately in their own villages. They were especially friendly with the French and the two often intermarried.

April 10, 1790 - Gamelin Encounters Kickapoo Warriors

Gamelin's party met thirteen Kickapoo warriors traveling to war, however they were not going to war with the settlers. After some discussion, the warriors promised not to steal from the whites. Gamelin gave them the speeches from St. Clair and asked them to go to the Chief of the Falls (St. Clair), shake hands and agree to peace. The Kickapoo said that they would do as he asked.

April 11, 1790 - Gamelin Visits Kickapoo Village

The day after encountering the Kickapoo warriors, Gamelin encountered a village of Kickapoo. This village had been as far as the first messenger had gotten before turning around and returning to Vincennes. Some disagreement between the interpreter and the village chief had made it impossible for the messenger to proceed. Gamelin presented the chief with two branches of white wampum and the letters from St. Clair. Gamelin managed to smooth things over with the chief. As to the council at Vincennes, the chief would not answer him until he heard from the tribes that inhabited Quitepiconnae (Tippecanoe), who then allowed Gamelin to proceed up the Wabash to stop at Quitepiconnae to hold council.

April 14, 1790 - Gamelin Holds Council with Wea and Kickapoo Indians

Antoine Gamelin held council at Ouiatenon with the combined peoples of the Kickapoo and Wea tribes. The natives were friendly with the Frenchman; however, their attitude towards the Americans was not so civil. After Gamelin delivered his speech, the chiefs told him that his admonishment to them to stop the young men from raiding settlements was impossible to carry out. The British were encouraging the attacks, thus the chiefs had little power over them. The chiefs told him that they could make no agreement without knowing the disposition of the Miamis at Kekionga. Thus, they invited him to travel on to that village and hold council there.

April 18, 1790 - Harmar Begins Scioto Campaign

Harmar and Governor Arthur St. Clair planned to strike at Kekionga later in the summer of 1790. Harmar wanted to run a campaign combining Kentucky militia and regular US Army troops as a "practice run" for this later campaign. The smaller campaign would accomplish two things, Harmar hoped. It would allow militia and army troops to learn to work together and clear the raiding Indians from the mouth of the Scioto River and stops the raids. A number of Kentucky militia units rendezvoused at Lexington Kentucky on April 15, marched to Limestone and crossed the Ohio. General Josiah Harmar's force departed Limestone on April 18. The force marched to a point on the upper waters of the river and then swept south along the river. Unfortunately, the natives at the camp learned of Harmar's force coming down the river and fled the camp before Harmar's men arrived. General Scott and many of his associates developed distaste for Harmar's leadership style and vowed never to participate in a campaign with him again. Thus, Harmar's fall campaign would be without many of the key militia units from Kentucky that could help it succeed.

April 24, 1790 - Gamelin Begins Council at Kekionga

Antoine Gamelin arrived at the Indian town of Kekionga on April 23. The next day, after giving each tribe two strands of wampum, he spoke to an assemblage of Chaouanons (Shawnee), Miami and Delaware. The chiefs had invited several French and English traders to attend the meeting. Gamelin gave the speeches given him by Governor St. Clair. When he concluded talking, he showed the chiefs a copy of the Treaty of Fort Harmar, concluded in January 1789. The appearance of the treaty displeased the Indians until Gamelin informed them that his purpose was not to sign another treaty, but to try to achieve peace among their peoples. The talks ended on a dubious note.

Meeting with Blue Jacket

The next day, the 25th, the Shawnee chief Blue Jacket invited Gamelin to his house where they discussed the situation in private. He indicated that the chiefs were pleased with Gamelin's speech, but were concerned because the Americans had deceived them before. He proposed giving the strands of wampum back to him and asking him to travel on to Detroit to talk to the commander of that post, because the natives would not give an answer until consulting with the British.

Meeting With Chief Le Gris

On the 26th, Gamelin reported the arrival of some Pottawattamie warriors with two Negroes they had captured. They sold these to some of the English traders present in the village. On the 27th, Gamelin met with Chief Le Gris. Le Gris was one of the three important chiefs of the Miami and had his dwelling at Kekionga. He had remained loyal to the British during the American Revolution and still maintained that loyalty. Lagro, Indiana derives its name from Chief Le Gris. During their discussions, Le Gris maintained that the Shawnee had acted contrary to his wishes. The meeting ended, however, the next day Le Gris met with him again. He said that Gamelin could return to Vincennes when he pleased, however he could not give him an answer to his request for a meeting at that post until he had sent copies of St. Clair's speech to Detroit and all the tribes in the Great Lakes region. He promised that within thirty days he would send a delegation of young men from each tribe to Vincennes with an answer.

Second Meeting with Blue Jacket

Blue Jacket invited Gamelin to his house for supper after Gamelin's meeting with Le Gris and during the course of the meal maintained that he thought that Gamelin should continue on to Detroit to consult with the British commander. Gamelin demurred, saying he would give his answer the next day.

Second Council

Gamelin called the chiefs to a second council on April 29th during which he said that he had nothing to say to the British commander at Detroit and that the commander would have nothing to say to him, so he would not go to Detroit. Blue Jacket rose to say that it was not his intention to force Gamelin to travel to Detroit and that the proposal was only a suggestion. He agreed with Chief Le Gris suggestion to consult with the other Great Lakes tribes and send an answer to Vincennes within thirty days. At the conclusion of the meeting, Blue Jacket once again invited Gamelin to supper.

Private Meeting with Blue Jacket

During this meeting, Blue Jacket indicated that the Shawnee did not recognize the treaty signed at Fort Harmar in January because the natives that signed it had done it in secret. These men were not chiefs and did not represent the Shawnee, or any of the other tribes. He also indicated that he did not trust St. Clair, as he had deceived the tribes before. Blue Jacket further said that if the whites did not stay off the north side of the Ohio River, there would never be peace, as the whites were stealing their hunting grounds and taking their women.

Gamelin Takes his Leave

After his discussions with the natives at Kekionga, Gamelin began his return on April 30.

May 01, 1790 - Father Gibault Sends Letter Requesting Land to Government

Father Pierre Gibault had incurred many expenses in his quest to aid George Rogers Clark capture Cahokia and Vincennes for which he had not received any compensation. Thus, on May 1, 1790 he dispatched a letter to Governor Arthur St. Clair requesting a small piece of land in Cahokia.

Request Dead End

Father Gibault, in aiding Clark, had enraged his fellow priests who had remained loyal to the British throughout the Revolutionary War. The British were also aware of his actions at Kaskaskia and Vincennes and did not want him back in their dominions. Thus, he was not welcome in Quebec. With few funds to maintain himself, Gibault had requested a transfer to Quebec. The request was denied. Thus, in desperation, he sent the letter to St. Clair. The request went unanswered, thus Gibault left Cahokia sometime after 1790. The last records of Gibault indicate he gave missions in the Arkansas region and probably died in or near New Madrid.

May 17, 1790 - Gamelin Returns to Vincennes

Gamelin began his journey home around April 30. On the return journey down the Wabash, he stopped at the villages that he had visited on his trip up the river. At two of the villages, he learned that the chiefs could not stop the young men from going to war. The Kickapoo village was nearly deserted, as the people were away on a hunting expedition; however, he learned that one of the more respected warriors had a "bad heart," and would not listen to the chiefs. Gamelin returned to Vincennes on May 17, where he filed his report with General Josiah Harmar.

June 20, 1790 - Knox County Organized - Parts of Illinois, Indiana, Ohio and Michigan

Knox County

Knox County was the third county organized as part of the Northwest Territory in 1790. The first three counties were Washington County, organized in 1788 and Hamilton County, organized in January 1790 and Knox on June 20, 1790. The original territory encompassed by Knox County included the current states of Indiana, Michigan, Illinois, and Ohio. The county takes its name from Henry Knox, the United States Secretary of War at the time the county was formed. Vincennes

Henry Knox (July 25, 1750 – October 25, 1806)

The son of William and Mary Campbell Knox, Henry was a native of Boston. He attended the Boston Latin School until his father died when he was twelve years old. Henry quit school to support his mother, taking a job at a bookstore. The bookstore owner, Nicholas Bowes, took a liking to the boy and served as a surrogate father to him, allowing him to take books from the store's stock home for him to read and then return. Military history, artillery and engineering books fascinated the boy and these dominated his reading. The knowledge he gained from studying these books would play a major role in his later life and career.

Militia and Patriot

In 1766, at 16 years old, Knox joined an artillery militia unit called The Train. As tensions between the colonists and the British increased in the years before the Revolutionary War, he became involved with the Sons of Liberty. He was a witness to the Boston Massacre in 1770 and played a minor role when he tried to diffuse the situation beforehand and testified during the soldier's trial. He opened his own bookstore in 1771, an endeavor that proved quite successful until the Boston Port Act closed the port in 1774. In 1772, he helped found a militia group called Boston Grenadier Corps. He served as the second on command of this group. A year later, he accidentally shot two of his fingers off with a gun. He managed to bind the wound and stop the bleeding until he found a doctor that could stitch the wound. Knox played at least a minor role in the Boston Tea Party by serving as a guard the night before the incident to ensure no one removed any tea from the ship.

Marriage and Exile

Knox married Lucy Flucker on June 16, 1774. It was an unlikely marriage, as Knox by this time was a committed patriot firmly opposed to British policy and an active resistor to the British. Lucy was the daughter of the Royal Secretary of the Province of Massachusetts. Her parents naturally opposed the union and her father tried, unsuccessfully, to have Henry enlist in the British Army, as Lucy's brother had. The couple would have thirteen children, ten of which would not survive childhood. When the Battles of Lexington and Concord broke out, Knox abandoned his bookstore and joined the gathering forces of Americans outside the city. Lucy accompanied him, sewing his sword inside the lining of her coat to conceal it from British guards stationed outside the city. After he fled loyalists looted his bookstore and stole the entire stock.

Siege of Boston

Knox joined the militia, serving under General Artemas Ward. The years he spent reading artillery and military engineering books now came to good use as he helped Ward design the fortifications around Boston. He also took part in the Battle of Bunker Hill in June by handling the colonial artillery.

Meeting with George Washington

George Washington had arrived in Cambridge to take command of the Continental Army on July 3, 1775. On July 5, he went on an inspection tour of the fortifications and met Knox, who was working on them. Washington and Knox took an instant liking to each other and Washington soon took him on in an unofficial role as an advisor on artillery.

Fort Ticonderoga Cannon

Knox recommended to General Washington that they end the siege of Boston by acquiring the cannon that Ethan Allen had captured at Fort Ticonderoga in May. Washington favored the difficult task and charged Knox with carrying it out. Knox began his quest in November 1775 and returned to Cambridge with the cannon by March 1776. Using the cannon, Washington forced the British to depart from Boston. The British would never return to New England.

The Remainder of the War

Knox remained a valuable asset to General Washington for the remainder of the Revolutionary War. He fought at Brandywine and Germantown and was present at Valley Forge where he assisted General Von Steuban drill the troops. Knox was also at Yorktown when Washington's army forced British General Cornwallis to surrender.

After the War

After the war, Congress appointed him as the second Secretary of War, a position he held until 1794.

For dining, lodging and shopping information in Knox County, visit:

Vincennes/Knox County Visitors and Tourism

779 South 6th Street

Vincennes, IN, 47591

(812)886-0400

(800)886-6443

July 15, 1790 - General Harmar Outlines His Battle Plan Against Kekionga

The Miami village of Kekionga loomed large in the battle plans of the United State government in the years 1789 and 1790 and on July 15, 1790 General Josiah Harmar outlined his plan to attack the village in a letter to Vincennes commander Jean François Hamtramck.

Kekionga

Located at the junction of the St. Mary's and St. Joseph River, the Miami village of Kekionga served as the principal village of the Miami tribe. At this spot, the two rivers form the headwaters of the Maumee River, which connects the region with Lake Erie. The current Indiana city of Fort Wayne currently occupies the site of the former village, which was located approximately between East State Boulevard and the junction of the three rivers in the neighborhood called Lakeside. The area contained a collection of Miami villages, known collectively as "the Miami Towns" or Miamitown. Kekionga occupied a strategic position as it connected with Lake Erie via the Maumee River. Cultivated fields of mostly corn that provided food for the natives surrounded Kekionga.

Important Portage

The Little River was only six miles to the south. The Little River's mouth is in the Wabash River, thus providing a convenient water route connecting Lake Erie with the Gulf of Mexico, via the Ohio and Mississippi Rivers. The portage between the Maumee/St. Mary's/St. Joseph was a valuable asset to European fur traders as they traveled between regions.

Trading and Agricultural Site

The British, still in possession of Detroit, considered the village an important trading site that produced over 2,000 packs of fur pelts for English traders. The Miami, according to estimates made by American Major Ebenezer Denny, who mapped the area during the campaign, had over 500 acres of cornfields near and around the village. The Miami would spend winters in their various winter hunting camps, gather at Kekionga during the spring to plant crops, and plan their war campaigns. During the winter months French and British fur traders that still occupied the area would live in the natives huts during the winter months when the Miami was in their winter hunting camps. Many of the French had intermarried with the Miami, providing many French surnames for the resulting children. These included the names Richardville, Lafontaine, and Rivarre. Other tribes, including the Huron, the Ottawa, and Shawnee met at the site, also. The village had become a major center for native attacks against the American settlements and thus provided an attractive target for the American military.

Harmar's Plan

President Washington, Secretary of War Henry Knox and Harmar had begun planning the campaign during the winter of 1789. President Washington authorized the plan and allowed Harmar a free hand in planning it. Harmar's plan was to have Major Jean François Hamtramck depart from Vincennes in late September and march up the Wabash. This was only a diversionary action, meant to distract the Miami from the main attack, which Harmar would launch from Fort Washington in early October. Their plans laid, the officers began making preparations. Harmar also fulfilled a requirement of the peace treaty with Britain by dispatching a messenger to Detroit informing the British commander there of the expedition. He did this in direct violation of President Washington's orders.

July 23, 1790 - The Intercourse Act

The United States Congress passed "An Act to Regulate Trade and Intercourse with the Indian Tribes," which was the first of several laws designed to regulate United States citizens within Indian Territory.

Purpose of the Act

Congress' intentions were to set up an orderly system of land acquisition from the various tribes and establish a process in which to sell those lands to Americans as the nation expanded west. The United States government needed revenue and wanted to use the land acquired from the native tribes by treaty as a revenue source. The United States Government would acquire the lands by negotiating treaties with native tribes, survey it and then sell it through land offices to pioneers, who would then settle on the land and establish homesteads.

Basics of the Law:

Require Americans to purchase a license from an authorized superintend appointed by the government

Authorized confiscation of goods meant for trade found with someone in Indian Territory who did not have a license

Forbade the sale of lands directly to Americans by the tribes

Established the authority of the government to negotiate treaties with the tribes to acquire their land

Directed that persons committing crimes in Indian Territory that lay within the jurisdiction of a state or territory were subject to the same penalties as if they committed them in the state or territory

Authorized removal of people that committed crimes and transport to a place within the state or territory for trial

Expiration of the act was to be two years after its passage

September 26, 1790 - Harmar's Force Leaves Fort Washington

Secretary of War Henry Knox had requested in mid August that Virginia and Pennsylvania raise a force of militia to conduct the operation. The states responded by recruiting about 1500 militiamen. Knox allocated 300 of these to Hamtramck's diversionary force and the remainder to Harmar, who was conducting the main thrust of the attack. The men that arrived at Fort Washington appeared to be mostly new immigrants. These men were unused to life on the frontier and did now know how to handle a gun. Indeed, many did not have guns. It seemed that many of the men conscripted to serve in the militia had paid recent immigrants to take their place in the campaign. There was no time to train the militia, as they had not assembled until September and Harmar wanted to complete the operation before winter set in. In addition, Harmar had about 320 regulars of the First American Regiment.

The Force Departs

The first elements of this force departed from Fort Washington on September 26. The remainder would follow on September 29. In addition to the approximately 1500 soldiers, the expedition included three six-pound cannon and a multitude of packhorses to carry the supplies the army needed. The packhorses would graze on whatever available grass they could find as they proceeded.

September 27, 1790 - The State of the Natives

By 1790, the native tribes in the Northwest Territory were on the defensive. Settlements in Kentucky and Ohio had reduced their hunting and farming lands, forcing them to move further west. With their way of life threatened, the Miami, Shawnee and other tribes fought a desperate war of survival. They enjoyed certain advantages in this fight. They knew the forests intimately and could disappear at will into their depths. Their savage tactics demoralized their white antagonists. However, they depended upon whites for their gunpowder and guns. The leaders lacked the power to compel any of the men to fight and when they did fight, they fought as individuals and not as a group. They preferred smaller, mobile wars as opposed to large ones. With their populations in decline, the natives could only form a large force was by forming alliances with other tribes. With no centralized command structure, the natives faced unfavorable odds in their long-term struggle against the whites, who wanted their lands. Two native leaders did rise to lead the resistance to the whites, Blue Jacket and Little Turtle.

Little Turtle (Michikinikwa) (c. 1747 – July 14, 1812),

The son of son of the Miami chief Acquenacke and a Mahican mother sometime n 1747, Little Turtle was native to a village in Whitley County, Indiana. The Miami tribe lists his birth in a village near Devil's Lake. Most consider him the Last Chief of the Miami Tribe. Historians know little of his early life. Little Turtle stood about six feet tall, disdained liquor and liked to wear silver on his clothing and ears.

War Chief

Little Turtle never became the head chief of the Miami, as this was a hereditary position. He became the war chief of the Miami tribe's Atchatchakangouen division through his prowess as a warrior. He led several raids against the French and Americans during the American Revolution. He gained his reputation as a warrior and leader during the October 1780 raid against Frenchman Augustin de La Balme, a battle known as La Balme's Defeat...

Little Turtle's War

After the Revolution, Little Turtle led the resistance against the encroaching Americans. Many of the western tribes joined in the Western Confederacy of tribes. Little Turtle emerged as the leader of this Confederacy. The Shawnee chief Blue Jacket also served as one of the leaders. Historians also call the war that arose from the conflict between the united tribes and the Americans as the Northwest Indian War.

Blue Jacket (Weyapiersenwah) (c. 1743 – 1810)

Historians know little about his early life. Speculation exists that he was born along the Guyan River in the Wyoming Valley of present-day West Virginia. His boyhood given name was Sepettekenathe (Big Rabbit) Upon reaching manhood, Sepetteken, as was custom among the Shawnee, chose the name Wayweyapiersenwaw (Whirlpool). Legend has it the name "Blue Jacket," arose from his habit of wearing a blue military coat that he had cut the arms out of. At adulthood, he stood about six feet tall with fine proportions and a muscular build. He probably matured during the raids the Shawnee conducted against the Americans in the early 1760's when the tribe ran out of ammunition and raided settlements to replenish their supplies. Blue Jacket was a leader during Lord Dunmore's War (1774). At the time, he enters this story he was already a proven war chief in the habit of wearing a silver gorgot (throat covering) and a large gold medallion bearing the image of King George III. He was married and had two sons that had received British education.

War and Relocation

The Shawnee had taken up arms against the Americans during the American Revolution. The village Blue Jacket belonged to moved from their home along the Scioto River in current southern Ohio. Sometime around 1777 Blue Jacket led a group of Shawnee to a site near present day Bellefontaine, Ohio, called "Blue Jacket's Town". During the Revolution and the years after, Blue Jacket led his tribe in almost constant warfare to attempt to keep their homes in Ohio and their hunting grounds in Kentucky and southern Indiana. A group of Kentucky militiamen, led by Benjamin Logan, destroyed Blue Jacket's Town in October 1786 during an expedition called Logan's Raid. The Shawnee then took up resident in a village somewhere along the Maumee River.

September 28, 1790 - The State of the Army

When the Constitution went into effect, the United States Army had less than 700 soldiers. President Washington had appointed Arthur St. Clair, who had had a mediocre career in the Army during the Revolutionary War, as commander of this force. When the troubles in the Northwest Territory with the native tribes accelerated, St. Clair prevailed upon Washington to increase the troops by asking Pennsylvania and Virginia to call out their militias to buttress the United

States Army forces. Congress, who had heard the rumors of increased attacks and bloodshed on the frontier, gave President Washington the authority to increase the numbers of United States Army soldiers to 1216. Both Congress and the President were unsure of the new Constitution's status of allowing a permanent standing army, thus both bodies of the government were reluctant to create a large military. These two states complied with the request and sent the required numbers.

No Training and Inadequate Supplies

Pennsylvania, Kentucky and Virginia had supplied 1500 militia to reinforce St. Clair's 320 regular Army troops. St. Clair had assigned 330 to Hamtramck for his use in the Vincennes portion of the campaign. These militiamen had received little in the way of training. Many did not even have weapons and of those that did, many did not know how to properly load and fire it. Many of the weapons they did bring were in poor repair. Some of the soldiers were recent immigrants from overseas. The army had not yet developed a dependable supply system. Thus, many of the suppliers were corrupt and did not deliver the needed supplies in a timely manner, if they delivered them at all. The late start of the expedition guaranteed that the horses and cattle accompanying the expedition would have little or no grass for grazing. It was with this force that St. Clair sent off to battle the desperate natives of Kekionga.

September 28, 1790 - The State of the Settlers

Disputes over payment of debts and confiscated properties owed to former British loyalists led Britain to retain six forts in United States Territory that the Treaty of Paris required them to abandon. Many English, including many in the British Army, believed that the American government was doomed to fail. Thus, they reasoned, when the United States fell, British troops would be in a position to move in and regain their lost colonies. These forts included:

Northwest Territory

Fort Miamis in northern Ohio

Fort Mackinac

Fort Lernoult, aka Fort Detroit

New York

Fort Niagara

Fort Oswegatchie

For Ontario

The British used many of these outposts, especially Fort Detroit, to foment problems with the natives in the Northwest Territory. In 1790, the population of the Northwest Territory stood at around 4,280, a number that included Negro slaves. In the six years before, over 1500 settlers had died at the hands of the Shawnee. Letters of the settlers to friends and relatives in the east relating the conflict with the natives discouraged settlement. In order to encourage settlement of the territory, St. Clair had to deal with the Indian threat. Historians estimate that the number of children captured by natives had been around 2,000. The natives had also stolen about 15,000 horses, destroyed cabins, and other structures. By 1786, about 400 Americans inhabited the southern regions of Indiana, mostly concentrated around Vincennes.

September 30, 1790 - Hamtramck Departs Vincennes

Major Jean François Hamtramck gathered about 330 militiamen and departed Fort Knox at Vincennes on his diversionary mission on September 22, 1790. The force rowed up the Wabash River to the villages located at the mouth of the Vermillion River. These villages Hamtramck found deserted, as the natives had seen their approach. The troops, subsisting on half rations, mutinied when Hamtramck ordered them to go further upriver. Hamtramck decided to return to Vincennes. Unknown to him at the time, 600 warriors waited in ambush just upriver. With his departure, these warriors would now have time to travel to Kekionga to participate in the Miami victories over Harmar, Hardin and Hartshorn.

October 16, 1790 - General Harmar Arrives at Kekionga

On October 14, a patrol captured a Shawnee warrior. Under interrogation, the warrior informed Harmar that Miami and Shawnee warriors were gathering at Kekionga to fight Harmar's army. The army continued its course until on October 16 the force entered the first of the Miami towns at the headwaters of the Maumee. Harmar's men found the village deserted, as the natives had fled. The found the other five villages deserted, also. The Miami had learned of Harmar's approach, possibly from information supplied by the British at Detroit, and fled, taking with them as much food and supplies that they could carry. British traders with ties to Detroit had been living in the villages with their families. The traders and their families left before Harmar arrived. As they departed, they gave the Miami all the guns and ammunition they had at their disposal. The traders also imparted information regarding the size of Harmar's force as well as intelligence regarding Harmar's inclination to drink heavily.

Destruction of the Towns

The soldiers, finding no enemy to fight, set on the task of destroying the native's food supply. They burned over 300 of the native's log houses and wigwams, destroyed hundreds of bushels of corn and vegetables. Meanwhile, in the lands surrounding Kekionga, hundreds of warriors waited for an opportunity to attack the Americans.

October 19, 1790 - Battle of Heller's Corner

United State Army forces under the command of Colonel John Hardin met an Amerindian force at Heller's Corner, near Fort Wayne, in battle. The native tribes dealt the Americans a terrible defeat.

John Hardin (Oct 1, 1753 - circa May 1792)

The son of Martin Hardin and Lydia Waters, John was native to Elk Run, Virginia. The family moved to George's Creek, Pennsylvania in 1765. Growing up on the frontier provided Hardin with an education in the ways of the woods, and he became an expert in the art of woodcraft. He put those skills to use in the 1774 Lord Dunmore's War and later with Daniel Morgan's Rifle Corps during the Revolutionary War. Hardin saw plenty of action during the Northwest Indian Wars in the Northwest Territory. In the future state of Indiana Hardin led strikes against the natives near Vincennes in 1786 and to Terre Haute in 1789. After the Battle of Heller's Corner, Hardin would die in May 1792 in an ambush while on a special mission for President George Washington.

Battle of Heller's Corner

Harmar sent Hardin out on October 15 with about 200 men to scout the area. This force consisted of about 30 United States regular troops and about 170 militiamen. A single warrior appeared in front of the force, which the soldiers began to pursue. Lured by the decoy, Hardin's rode into an ambush in swampy lowlands near the Eel River. The natives killed twenty-two of the regulars and forty militiamen. Some refer to the battle as Hardin's Defeat. Many credit Miami Chief Little Turtle with leading the attack, however there is conflicting evidence that he did.

October 20, 1790 - Hartshorn's Defeat

The day after the Battle of Heller's Corner, General Josiah Harmar sent Ensign Phillip Hartshorn out with 300 soldiers. About eight miles from Kekionga, a large band of warriors ambushed the troops. In the ensuing battle twenty soldiers died, including Hartshorn. The natives forced the soldiers to make a hasty defeat, leaving their dead exposed on the field of battle. Harmar refused to allow a burial detail to retrieve the bodies and retreated further from Kekionga. Having experienced two battles in two days that ended in defeat and the abandonment of their comrades on the battlefield, the army's morale dropped. However, the worst was yet to come.

Events of 1791

January 02, 1791 - Attack at Big Bottom - Muskingum River

A surprise attack by a band of about twenty-five Wyandot and Delaware warriors attacked a new settlement sponsored by the Ohio Company at Big Bottom, on the east bank of the Muskingum River, near Fort Harmar.

New Settlements

The construction of new forts along the Ohio River was supposed to keep new settlers from entering the lands north of the Ohio River, as the troops stationed there were required to evict people that settled illegally on native lands. The presence of the forts instead had the opposite effect, as the presence of the new forts appeared to offer some protection to any settlement that located nearby. The Ohio Company of Associates sponsored several new settlements along the river, one of which was a settlement called Big Bottom on the east bank of the Muskingum River about thirty miles north of its mouth with the Ohio River.

Big Bottom

The Ohio Company allocated land to new settlers in the tracts they controlled with the expectation that the new owners would settle there and make improvements to the property. Much of this land was located in lands still owned by the native tribes. This was the case with Big Bottom, which the settlers established along a major trail used by the tribes to travel from the area around Sandusky, Ohio to the Muskingum River. In December 1790 a group of about thirty-six settlers constructed a blockhouse at the site, followed a month later by a couple of cabins. The new settlement soon attracted the attention of some natives, with predictable results.

The Attack

The warriors had reconnoitered the new settlement in late December. On January 2, 1791, sometime between dawn and dusk, they attacked Big Bottom. The settlers had not posted any sentries, thus the attack caught them by surprise. The natives killed thirteen people, including men, one woman and two children that had taken refuge in the blockhouse. They took one teen-age boy captive. The warriors next attacked a cabin that stood a short distance north of the blockhouse and captured the four inhabitants. At another cabin to the south, the two people escaped into the forest, avoiding capture. The natives stacked the dead bodies in the blockhouse and set it on fire. The fire burned out before consuming the bodies. On January 4, a rescue party appeared to find the burned out blockhouse and the charred remains. They also found an Indian war club hanging nearby, a symbol that the natives had declared war on the settlers. After the attack, the settlement was abandoned.

October 22, 1790 - Battle of Pumpkin Fields

Harmar spent October 21 berating his militia, who had failed to perform in the previous day's battle, and burning the remainder of the villages near Kekionga. Harmar still wanted to deal the natives a decisive military defeat so he sent Major John Wyllys in command of 300 regulars into Kekionga.

Planned Ambush

Wyllys, a Revolutionary War veteran, decided to attempt to trap the Indians between two detachments of his force. Before dawn, he sent one part to cross the Maumee River near the town while another part was to cross the St. Joseph

River to block the Indians defeat when they retreated from the attack of the first force.

Little Turtle Springs His Own Ambush

Little Turtle saw what the Americans had planned and devised his own trap. He had plenty of warriors available, as news of the two victories had spread among the tribe, bringing more warriors into the area. Little Turtle had one band of natives attack the soldiers as they crossed the Maumee, hitting them with musket fire as they crossed the river. The second detachment that was supposed to cross the St. Joseph heard the battle sounds and quickly joined the first group. When these soldiers appeared and Wyllys force continued crossing the Maumee, the first decoy band of warriors broke off the attack and ran. The Americans, sensing victory, pursued the running warriors and ran into Little Turtle's real ambush. In the ensuing battle, about 183 Americans died, about thirteen percent of the force. Wyllys also died in the assault. The natives lost around forty warriors. The Americans, badly stung, retreated, leaving their dead and many wounded behind.

Battle of the Pumpkin Fields

The natives called this the Battle of the Pumpkin fields because the steam rising off freshly scalped skulls in the cool morning air reminded them of pumpkins in a misty autumn morning field. The only thing that saved Harmar's army from total defeat was the occurrence of an eclipse of the Harvest Moon that evening. The Indians, who with their superior numbers and morale, could have crushed the American army in a final blow. The natives interpreted the eclipse as a bad omen and believed that if they attacked, they would lose many warriors. Therefore, they did not attack and Harmar's army retreated to Fort Washington.

Joseph Boone

A nephew of Daniel Boone, Joseph, took part in the battle as part of the force that was to swing around the St. Joseph River. Early in the battle, he was shot in the ankle. Disabled, Boone lay on the battlefield. In the excitement of battle, several braves passed by him without scalping him. Two militiamen saw Boone, dragged him from the field, and hid him in a tangle of branches and logs near the river. In the evening they left him to go to the main force still camped nearby to get help. In severe pain, Boone slaked his thirst in the river and waited. The men did return, however Boone feared they were Indians and did not reveal his position. The militiamen, not finding him, were about to give up the search. One of them spoke; Boone recognized the voice and cried out. They found him and dragged him back to the main camp. Boone survived and in 1794 married Rebecca Fry-Lock, with whom he would have three children.

November 03, 1790 - Remainders of Harmar's Force Returns Fort Washington

General Josiah Harmar and his decimated force returned to Fort Washington on November 3, 1790. He had marched out of the fort with 320 Federal troops and 1453 militia. The troops suffered forty killed at the Battle of Heller's Corner, twenty at Hartshorn's Defeat and 129 men at the Battle of the Pumpkin Fields. 1,584 soldiers filed back into the fort, having suffered 189 killed in battle and over one hundred wounded.

Public Outrage

When the defeat became known, outrage against Harmar swept across the young nation, as Harmar became a scapegoat for the humiliating defeat. Harmar, to clear himself of charges of on various charges of negligence, requested a court martial, which he received. The court cleared him of wrongdoing. He resigned his commission on January 1, 1792.

Adjutant General

After his resignation, he returned to his estate near Philadelphia on the Schuylkill River, which he called "The Retreat." Pennsylvania would appoint him as adjutant general of the Pennsylvania militia. He married Sarah ("Sally") Jenkins on October 19, 1784. The couple had four children. Harmar died on August 20, 1813 and is interred at the Episcopal Church of St. James, Kingsessing, in West Philadelphia.

December 30, 1790 - Virginia Governor Establishes Kentucky Board of War

The governor of Virginia, responding to political pressure from the beleaguered citizens of Kentucky, appointed General Scott as commander of the entire complement of militia in the District of Kentucky. On the same day, President George Washington accepted the recommendation of Congressman John Brown, Virginia congressman representing Kentucky that he set up a Board of War to deal with the Indian threat on the frontier.

District of Kentucky

The District of Kentucky was still technically part of Virginia, created by the Virginia legislature on December 07, 1776. That same year the Virginia Constitution created a process by which Kentucky could separate from Virginia. This process began with a convention on December 2, 1784. It would take nine more conventions to complete the process, which culminated by the admission of Kentucky as the fourteenth state on June 1, 1792. The Virginia assembly began paying its militia soldiers with land grants in western

Kentucky, which facilitated settlement when many of the soldiers migrated to the region to claim their land grants. By 1790 the creation of Nelson County (1784), and Bourbon, Madison, and Mercer had buttressed the original three counties of Fayette, Jefferson, and Lincoln in 1785. The first Federal census of Kentucky in 1790 reported 73,077.

Board of War

Washington appointed John Brown, Scott, Isaac Shelby, Harry Innes, and Benjamin Logan as members of this committee. The committee had the responsibility of calling out the local militia to respond to Indian attacks and to act in concert with Federal troops in any operations against them. The committee recommended the formation of an army of volunteers to deal with the threat. Scott sent letters to many of the Kentucky leaders about possibly establishing defensive posts along the Ohio River to defend against attacks.

Events of 1791

January 8, 1791 - Governor St. Clair Reaches Falls of the Ohio on Western Tour

Northwest Territory Governor Arthur St. Clair embarked on a tour of the Western portion of the Northwest Territory from the Territory's capital at Marietta. He left in the winter of 1789 to organize local governments in the vast territory. The citizens of the newly formed territory clamored for some governmental organization.

Losantiville

Around January 1 the party departed Losantiville, which St. Clair had renamed Cincinnati and traveled by boat down the Ohio River, arriving at the Great Falls of the Ohio on January 8, 1790.

Arrival at the Great Falls

He arrived with the Territory's Secretary, Winthrop Sargent and the Territory's Supreme Court judges. After his arrival, St. Clair authorized a temporary local government at Clarksville. He appointed William Clark Justice of the Peace and captain of the Militia. They visited Fort Finney, later renamed Fort Steuben in 1791.

January 08, 1791 - Surveyors Attacked near Dunlap's Station

A band of Shawnee warriors attacked a small group of surveyors that were surveying and exploring some bottomland that lay near Fort Colerain, also known as Dunlap's Station.

Colerain Earthwork

Early in 1790, a surveyor named John Dunlap platted a town, first called Dunlap's Station and later Fort Colerain. The new settlement lay on the east side of the Great Miami River. The river at this point bends to the west, and then curves back east forming a "U" shaped tract of floodplain that early settlers would have coveted as farmland. Currently the Dunlap Station Cemetery at nearly the center of the tract on East Miami River Road is all that remains of this early settlement near Heritage Park. A large "D" shaped earthworks dating from the Hopewell Era (approximately 200 AD to 400 AD) was adjacent to the fort. Called the 2,000-year-old Colerain Earthwork, the structure had nine-foot tall walls and was about ninety-five feet in diameter. Located within the structure were one or more Adena Indian Mounds.

Dunlap's Station

A group of Irish settlers led by surveyor John Dunlap settled into the area they called Colerain, after the region in Ireland from which they originated. The constructed a small fort, cleared some of the land and began farming. The built some cabins and enclosed them in a wooden stockade that was about eight feet high. The stockade surrounded the cabins on three sides and fronted the deep river, which offered protection on that side. About thirty people lived in the settlement, of which only about ten of them were capable of defending the village. Nearby they erected a log blockhouse that would offer protection against Indian attack. As the year advanced, natives began gathering near the settlement, alarming the new settlers, who appealed to the commander of nearby Fort Washington for protection. General Harmar dispatched a twelve-man force led by a Lieutenant Kingsbury to occupy the fort. The soldiers had cannon, which they would use to terrify any native attackers.

The Attack

The site the surveyors had chosen to explore was about seventy yards from the fort. In the evening, a band of natives ambushed them and fired several volleys at them. The men's names were Wallace, Hunt, Cunningham, and Sloan. Cunningham died in the first volley and Sloan was wounded. The three surviving survivors fled, however Abner Hunt's horse threw him and the natives captured him. The rest managed to reach the fort's safety.

January 10 1791- Siege of Dunlap's Station

Two days after attacking the surveyors a band of 300 - 500 native warriors led by Blue Jacket and Simon Girty attacked Dunlap's Station.

Simon Girty (November 14, 1741 – February 18, 1818)

The son of Simon and Mary Newton Girty, Simon was native to Harrisburg, Pennsylvania. When Simon was about nine years old, his father died in a duel or fight. About three years later his father's half brother, John Turner, and his mother married. That marriage produced a son, John that joined Simon and his brothers Thomas, James and George. By the time the French and Indian War broke out the family had moved to a farm near Sherman's Creek in eastern Pennsylvania. Numerous Indian attacks in the area led the family to seek protection in nearby Fort Granville. Turner joined the militia as a sergeant.

Capture by Indians

A force of about 50 French soldiers and 100 Delaware warriors attacked the fort while a large contingent of the troops was out on patrol on August 2, 1756. The French set the stockade on fire, then killed several of the defenders as they fought the fire. John Turner was the acting commander of the fort while the commander was away on patrol. He surrendered the fort after the commander of the French force promised that no one would be killed. Thus, John Turner, his wife and family became prisoners of the Delaware.

Death of John Turner

Simon's father had worked as a trader among the natives, thus they recognized Mary, Simon and his brothers. They also recognized John Turner. Their idea was that he had engineered Simon Girty Senior's death so he could steal his wife, family and property. They also thought that he had killed or beaten an Indian. For one of these reasons or another unknown one, they condemned Turner to death. They tortured him for three hours by heating gun barrels to a red-hot temperature, then plunging them into his body while his wife and children watched. Then, either they burned him at the stake or a warrior killed him by tomahawking him in the head.

Life among the Seneca

After Turner's death, the Delaware split the family up with Simon ending up with the Mingoes, in a village near Lake Erie in northwestern Pennsylvania. The Mingo made Simon run the gauntlet, a practice that involved making a person run naked between two rows of natives who clubbed, stabbed at or hit the runner as they passed by. Simon ran this successfully, gaining the respect of the Mingo. Thus, at fifteen years old young Simon integrated with the Seneca, a lifestyle he grew to love. He remained among the Mingos until 1764, when Colonel Henry Bouquet demanded that the

Ohio Indians release all of their prisoners during negotiations near the end of Pontiac's War in 1764. Thus, in 1764 twenty-three year old Simon Girty rejoined white society after eight years among the Seneca. During his captivity, Girty had learned the Seneca language, some Delaware and Shawnee as well as several other native languages.

Murky History

Historians know little about his life during the next ten years. Many think he worked as a trader in the Ohio River valley. He served a valuable role several times, as his knowledge of native languages made him an asset as an interpreter during treaty meetings with British officials and he native tribes. During this time, he undoubtedly met and became friends with Simon Kenton, Daniel Boone and other frontier legends.

Revolution

Girty had served as a scout for the British during Lord Dunmore's War in 1774. When war broke out between the colonists and the British, he first sided with the colonists in the War of Independence. He operated out of Fort Pitt as a scout. After an ugly incident involving the killing of some defenseless Indians by American forces, Girty decided to defect to the British, who had tried to recruit him before as an interpreter and scout. Now helping the British with their plan of using the Indians to attack the Americans, he fought at the Battle of Blue Licks and the attack at Bryan's Station. Girty gained the nickname "White Savage", during this time because of his habit of wearing native attire and especially his presence during the torture of Colonel William Crawford in 1782. The rumor grew that he taunted the dying Crawford. His reputation as a ruthless killer of whites on the frontier became part of frontier lore. However, there are many reports of his saving other whites condemned to death by the natives. His path between the white world and the native one was not an easy one.

Northwest War

During the early stages of the Northwest Indian War, Girty continued to assist the natives in their struggles to oust the whites from their lands. The encounter at Dunlap's Station was one of the first encounters during that war.

The Siege

When the surveyors ran into the fort, Lieutenant Jacob Kingsbury knew that there were Indians about and began preparing for a siege. On the morning of January 10, the natives, dragging the captive Abner Hunt along, demanded that they settlers surrender or they would kill Hunt. Kingsbury refused to surrender the garrison. During the negotiations, gunfire broke out. The conflict continued for several hours with the warriors unsuccessfully attempting to set fire to the fort with fire arrows. The natives once again demanded that the garrison surrender and Kingsbury once again refused. Various conflicting reports say that Hunt died when the warriors built a fire on his abdomen. Kingsbury's report after the siege does not mention it; however, Hunt did die during the encounter. The fighting ended after dark; however, it began early the next morning. Around 8:00 AM, the natives departed. At around 10:00 a rescue expedition arrived from Fort Washington.

March 03, 1791 - Congress Approves Enlargement of the Army

The weak link in the chain for the military was the use of militias, thus the Congress passed an act on March 3, 1791 that authorized President Washington to raise one additional regiment to fight the threat on the frontier.

Increasing Threat

The natives, especially the Shawnee and the Miami tribes that occupied the Ohio River Valley, had increased their raids against the settlements in the future states of Indiana, Ohio and Kentucky. Their defeat of General Josiah Harmar had both increased their confidence and their hope that they could evict the whites from their hunting and agricultural lands. The rumors of these raids filtered back to Washington, setting once again the debate about the wisdom and Constitutionality of establishing a large standing army.

The Debate

The Constitution had given the Federal Government the authority to establish an army and a navy, the ability to levy taxes to maintain the force and the means to establish a separate executive department to administer the military. The Founders had also given the President the position of Commander in Chief. In theory, the President could personally command the armed forces, or appoint a delegate to perform that service. The Constitution had given the Congress the power to declare war and provide the financial needs of the military, thus hoped to rein in any attempt by the military to seize control. Many in the Congress and President Washington had major concerns about the establishment of a permanent, large army. President Washington had observed that a large standing army in time of peace was "dangerous to the liberties of a country." The financial drain of creating and maintaining a large force was also an impediment to a new nation without the means to pay for it. The Constitution had also authorized the various states to control the recruitment and training for their militias. The states also had the ability to appoint the officers of this regiment. Since the states were also responsible for paying for these militias, many were reluctant to properly train, arm and equip a large militia force. The only federal control of these militias were the regulations and guidelines adopted by Congress.

Compromise

The various bills passed by Congress during the early years of the Republic attempted to bridge the gap between the Constitution, their own fears of a large standing army and the financial drain of doing so and the needs of the nation to defend itself. On March 3, the Congress passed a bill that authorized:

The raising of an additional regiment of 912 men

The appointment of officers to command this force

The ability to issue a levy or levies to buttress the regular army and militia, or to replace the militia force

Stipulated that the maximum length of service for these levies was to be six months

Authorized that the levies could total up to 2000 additional soldiers

Hopes for the Act

The President and Congress hoped that the Act would provide sufficient resources to deal with the threat in the Northwest Territory and allow the United States to secure the frontier.

March 04, 1791 - President Washington Appoints Arthur St. Clair Commander of Expedition

With the legislation authorization for increasing the army passed by Congress, President Washington needed a commander for the mission. He appointed the fifty-five year old, ailing Governor Arthur St. Clair as major general in charge of the operation. The Northwest Territorial governor, though he was in poor health, accepted the assignment.

March 04, 1791 - Samuel Hodgdon Appointed as Quartermaster General

Henry Knox appointed his former commissary of military stores officer from the Continental Army, Samuel Hodgdon, as Quartermaster General, serving under General Arthur St. Clair.

Samuel Hodgdon (September 3, 1745 - June 9, 1824)

The son of Benjamin and Rebecca Marshall Hodgdon, Samuel was native to Boston, Massachusetts. Historians know little of his early life. In 1776, He served as a lieutenant in the Continental Marines that had formed in November 1775. General Henry Knox appointed him as a Captain of Artillery in 1777 and later as principal field commissary of military stores. The Continental Congress appointed him as commissary general of military stores and as an assistant to the Quartermaster General, Thomas Pickering. As the war ended, Pickering and Hodgdon went into a mercantile business together on May 10, 1783. This business lasted about five years, however the men remained business associates for many more years. On July 20, 1785, the government abolished the Quartermaster General office, eliminating Hodgdon's job. On March 4, 1791, he assumed the position of Quartermaster General after President Washington had nominated him for the post and Congress concurred.

Quartermaster General

The Continental Congress created the Continental Army on June 14, 1775. Two days later, on June 16, 1775 they created the post of Quartermaster General and Deputy Quartermaster General. The men holding these positions held the responsibility of procuring all the supplies needed by the troops. This included food, clothing, horses, munitions and many other items. The Quartermaster General was also responsible for keeping supply lines in good repair, including the roads the supplies on which the supplies traveled. They acted as chief of staff for their commanding officer and dealt directly with the civilian merchants that supplied the goods to the army. The Quartermaster General during this era was a civilian. He received the pay and the privileges of a lieutenant colonel; however, he did not have the actual rank.

March 10, 1791 - Thomas Proctor Receives Commission for Peace Mission

President George Washington attempted to stave off war between the United States and the natives of the Wabash when he commissioned Secretary of War Henry Knox to make entreaties to the native tribes. On March 10, 1791, Knox contacted Colonel Thomas Procter and commissioned him to lead an expedition to hold a conference with the Indians to the Seneca chief Cornplanter's village in North Central Pennsylvania to hold a peace conference with the tribes.

Thomas Procter (c.1739 - March 16, 1806)

The son of Francis and Elizabeth Pratt Proctor, Thomas was native to Longford, County Longford, Ireland. His father, a carpenter by trade, moved the family to Philadelphia sometime before the American Revolution. On October 27, 1775, he received a commission as a Captain of Artillery from the Philadelphia Committee of Safety. Procter saw heavy action during the Revolutionary War serving at the Battle of Brandywine, the Battle of Germantown and endured the winter of Valley Forge with Washington's army. He rose in rank to Colonel of artillery on May 18, 1779. A disagreement with another officer led to his resignation in 1781. He gained election as the High Sheriff of Philadelphia in 1783, which he held until 1786. He received his commission as an ambassador to the Northwest natives on March 10, 1791.

March 12, 1791 - Thomas Proctor Departs on Peace Mission

Thomas Proctor departed from Philadelphia on March 12, 1791 on his mission to the natives accompanied by Captain Michael G. Houdin. Heavy rains had turned the roads into a quagmire of mud and soaked the travelers.

Secret Destination

Proceeding northeast, the men reached Reading, Pennsylvania on March 14, where Proctor opened his instructions from Secretary of War Henry Knox. He wanted to keep his instructions and ultimate destination unknown, even to his family, until he was well on the road.

Out of His Way

At Reading, he discovered that he was to go to Wilkesburg to pick up Captain Waterman Baldwin, in northeastern Pennsylvania first and thence to the Seneca chief Cornplanter's Village along the Allegheny River in North Central Pennsylvania. Thus, he had traveled fifty miles out of his way by traveling through Reading, which was to the southwest of Wilkesburg instead of taking the more direct route through Bethlehem, to the east. While at Reading, he also learned that General Arthur St. Clair was at Fort Washington along the Ohio River preparing for an expedition against the natives in the Wabash Valley.

Onward

From Reading, the company proceeded northwest on roads made nearly impassable by the heavy rains. They made a difficult crossing the flooded Little Schuylkill River on March 15 and the East Branch of the Susquehanna River by ferry near Northumberland on March 17.

Michael G. Houdin (? - February 1802)

Native to France, Michael G. Houdin migrated to the United States sometime around 1777 and was appointed as a lieutenant in the 15th Regiment, Massachusetts Infantry. Houdin served in the Northern Department where he fought at the Battles of Stillwater and Saratoga. He endured the winter at Valley Forge after which he participated in the Battle of Monmouth, the Siege of Newport and the Battle of Rhode Island. On June 28, June 28, 1779 he received a promotion to Captain. He retired with honors on January 1, 1784, after which he returned to France. Houdin came back to the United States in 1791 to live. He was appointed Captain and Deputy to the Quartermaster General in the United States Army. In 1801, he became the military storekeeper at Albany, New York until his death in 1802.

March 19, 1791 - Thomas Proctor Arrives at Wilkesburg

Thomas Proctor and Captain Houdin proceeded along the flooded Susquehanna about twelve miles, through the mountainous terrain.

Difficult Journey

They made a failed attempt to cross the river at a narrow spot; however, the raging waters almost carried the men and their horses away. They next ascended the summit of a steep precipice to reconnoiter. They decided to circumvent the mountain. They labored to travel through the difficult terrain, but could find no route through the ridge of mountains to proceed. Thus, they made their way back through the dense forest to the place they had started from that morning. They managed to get the ferryman to brave the flooded waters to carry them back across, which he did, with four other men assisting him.

Destination Reached

After shoeing one of the horses and eating dinner, the men proceeded along the hazardous mountain road towards Wilkesburg. At nine o'clock that night, they reached the village of Wyoming. They hired a guide to find lodging for the night and feed for the horses. They also acquired a tinderbox, and helved a tomahawk. Helving is the process of putting a new handle on a wooden handled tool. The next morning they departed Wyoming and arrived at Wilkesburg around eleven o'clock in the morning.

Tinderbox

Before matches came into use during the 1820's, people used tinderboxes to light fires, candles and cigars. A tinderbox was a small steel box that held the essentials of fire making, pyrite, flints, tinder and later on sulfur tipped matches.

Pyrite

Also called fool's gold because many inexperienced gold seekers confused the shiny, yellow colored mineral for gold, pyrite is a form of iron that casts a spark when a hard rock, like flint, strikes it. Pyrite also found use in early firearms as a source of the spark that lit the gunpowder in the chamber. Later tinderboxes used carbon steel instead of pyrite.

Flint

Flint is a hard sedimentary rock found in deposits of other sedimentary rocks like limestone and chalk. Flint's shiny color causes it to stand out among the other minerals among which it is typically found. Flint is harder than pyrite and causes the pyrite to cast a spark when struck against it. Other minerals used in tinderboxes include chert, quartz, agate, jasper or chalcedony.

Tinder

Early tinderboxes used a material called char cloth. Typically, pioneers made their own char cloth out of a piece of linen, cotton or jute. They put a small piece of the cloth in a tin box that had a small hole in the top. They then laid the box in the coals of a fire. In a process similar to making charcoal from wood, the hot coals converted the cloth into a material that had a low ignition point and would burn hot. When the box was first laid in the coals, the cloth would smolder, but not burn, as the tin box held very little of the oxygen needed for full combustion. When smoke ceased issuing from the small hole in the tin box, it was withdrawn from the coals. The char cloth would ignite easily from a tiny spark, creating a small fire that would ignite kindling. Sometimes people used frayed rope or other finely divided material. Dried mosses or fungal growths also served as tinder in time of need.

Sulfur Tipped Matches

A sulfur tipped match was a small stick of wood, usually pine, whose tip was impregnated with a small quantity of sulfur. Sulfur is easily ignited and when held against an already existing fire the match burst into flame, allowing it to be used to light candles, oil lamps or cigars.

Lighting a Fire

Before using the tinderbox, a person gathered a quantity of finely split kindling and laid it in a pile at the spot they wanted to build a fire. Next, they laid a quantity of char cloth or other tinder at the base of the kindling. They would then hold the pyrite close to the tinder and strike it sharply with the flint, which would cast a spark. The spark fell into the tinder, creating a small, smoldering fire. The person building the fire would then bend close and blow on the smoldering fire, coaxing it into flame, igniting the kindling. After the kindling began burning, they then added larger and larger pieces of wood until they had a fire. To light candles, lamps or cigars, they held the sulfur tipped matches against a coal, igniting it and then using the match to light the fire.

March 19, 1791 - General Charles Scott Receives Orders to Attack Fort Ouiatenon

Secretary of War Henry Knox issued orders to General Charles Scott to prepare to move against the natives at Ouiatenon. However, he was not to begin the mission until after May 10 to give Thomas Proctor a chance to complete his mission.

Charles Scott (April 1739 – October 22, 1813)

The son of Samuel Scott, Charles was native to Goochland (Powhatan) County, Virginia. His mother's name is unknown, she probably died sometime in 1845. He received his education from his parents until his father died in 1755, leaving the family farm to his older brother, John. He apprenticed to a carpenter and enlisted in the Virginia militia shortly before local authorities placed him in an orphanage.

French and Indian War

Scott served with the Braddock campaign to capture Fort Duquesne and performed well enough to rise steadily in the ranks, rising to ensign during the Forbes campaign that eventually captured that vital fort in 1757. He left the army in 1762 to take over the family farm, as his brother had passed away. He married Frances Sweeney, with whom he had nine or ten children.

Revolutionary War

At the beginning of the Revolutionary War, he raised a company of men and gained election as lieutenant colonel in

November 1775. He participated in several campaigns early in the war, and then took a furlough in 1777. Upon his return, General George Washington promoted him to brigadier general. He took part in the Battle of Brandywine, the Battle of Germantown and the Battle of Monmouth. He again took a furlough. He returned to begin a recruitment drive in Virginal after which Washington sent him to South Carolina. The British captured him after the Siege of Charleston in 1780. The British exchanged him in a prisoner swap later that year. He returned to duty as a recruiting officer, which he performed until war's end.

Kentucky

After the war, he settled in Kentucky and raised a company of militia to fight in the Northwest Indian Wars. He served under Arthur St. Clair in several campaigns and received assignment to Fort Steuben, near present day Clarkston, Indiana. At Fort Steuben, he and his company were discharged, but he returned to duty to join General Anthony Wayne and eventually took part in the Battle of Fallen Timbers. He returned to his farm in Kentucky and gained election as governor of Kentucky in 1808. He returned to his Canewood Estate near Frankfort, Kentucky where he died on October 22, 1813.

March 20, 1791 - Thomas Proctor Arrives at Captain Waterman Baldwin's Home

Proctor and Houdin arrived in the evening of March 20 at the home of Captain Waterman Baldwin, where they would spend two days.

Waterman Baldwin (January 7, 1757 - April 27, 1810)

The son of Son of Isaac Baldwin, Sr. and Patience Rathbun, Waterman was native to Norwich, New London Co., New York. In 1777, he enlisted in the 4th Connecticut Regiment, commanded by Captain Robert Durkee. The unit spent the winter at Valley Forge as part of Varnum's Brigade. The unit fought at the Battles of Philadelphia-Monmouth in June 1778 and the Battle of Yorktown. He later served in Captain William Spaulding's Wyoming Independent Company. He married Celinda Hazen, with whom he would have three children. Cornplanter had taken him prisoner by Cornplanter's warrior and held at Tonawanda Creek, which is near Niagara. He had been instrumental in the treaty the United States signed with Cornplanter. President Washington had commissioned him to be a teacher for Cornplanter's village and to help the natives learn the white men's agricultural practices.

March 21, 1791 - Secretary of War Knox Issues Orders for St. Clair's Campaign

Knox's orders to St. Clair were simple in concept. Assemble an army of 4000 soldiers, build a road from Fort Washington to Kekionga and establish a series of forts along this road to guard the supply line. At Kekionga St. Clair was to build a fort to awe the natives into submission and connect the chain of forts with a 150 mile long north/south road. St. Clair's orders advised him not to engage the natives; however, he was to use his force of men to convince the natives to stop attacking the frontier settlements. Knox also ordered him to make more treaties with them and force them to surrender more of their land.

March 22, 1791 - Proctor's Party Arrives at Buttermilk Falls

Proctor and his party traveled up the Susquehanna, passing the mouth of the Lackawanna River and arrived by nightfall at the mouth of Buttermilk Creek. They camped there for the night. Proctor had commanded a fleet of 214 ships on the Susquehanna River and had visited the site in 1779 during the Revolutionary War. His fleet carried the provisions and supplies for 6000 troops involved in an expedition commanded by General John Sullivan.

Buttermilk Falls

The falls, currently located on private property in Lackawanna County and Wyoming County, in Pennsylvania, provided the power for many gristmills in the area. The falls, currently located on private property in Lackawanna County and Wyoming County, in Pennsylvania, provided the power for many gristmills in the area. The beautiful falls cascade eighty feet from a six foot wide rock lip located on a mountain top.

Continuing the Journey

The next morning Proctor and his expedition had to leave the road that paralleled the river and go inland due to extreme flooding of the Susquehanna River and all of its tributaries.

March 26, 1791 - Proctor's Party Arrives at Tioga Point

The road Proctor and his party took from Buttermilk Falls was a new road, fresh cut through the deep hemlock forests. The first thirteen miles the travelers endured a steep incline over this road. The road was about twenty feet wide and littered with freshly cut trees that lay scattered across the road. Heavy rains, and at times snow, impeded their journey. They stopped to camp for the night at various farms and small settlements along the way, purchasing corn, oats for the horses and other supplies along the way.

Hawbottom

At one such settlement, called Hawbottom, they camped at a sugar camp, the owners of which had had the poor fortune of losing most of their supplies when a canoe overturned in the Lahawanock River two days prior. Proctor gave them such supplies as he could spare and moved on. They camped at a farmer named Richard McNemara on March 24, still about ten miles from Tioga Point. A heavy rain soaked them. The rain turned to snow overnight, coating the forest, and the road, with a fifteen-inch layer of snow.

Tioga Point

At Tioga Point Proctor and his party would travel west to the Genesee River, crossing the Tioga along the way. This was largely uninhabited land, so Proctor purchased a packhorse to carry supplies. Captain Baldwin also purchased a horse for his farming project with the Indians. Proctor hired a native guide called Cayautha, whose English name was Peter. The travelers now totaled three white men, one Indian and five horses. Food for both humans and horses had been scanty thus far and the men had walked most of the distance to save the horse's energy. The roads had been muddy from both rain and snow. The road to the Genesee was just a blind path through the forest. The journey would tax their resources of the exhausted men and horses further. On the morning of March 27, they set out for the Genesee.

April 8, 1791 - Proctor's Party Arrives at Fort Franklin

Proctor and his party traveled from Tioga Point northwest to Canaseder (Caneadea) and then southwest to an Indian village called Obhishew at the junction of Oil Creek and the Allegheny River. Along the way, they held several councils inviting the tribes to the conference at Buffalo Creek. Learning of a series of incidents that several of the natives had taken refuge in Fort Franklin, Proctor and his party traveled to the fort, arriving on April 8, 1791.

Fort Franklin

Constructed in 1781, the fort was about a half mile upstream from where French Creek empties into the Allegheny River in Pennsylvania. The garrison included about 100 officers and men. The post was abandoned in 1796.

April 08, 1791 - Cornplanter Visits Proctor Fort Franklin

Soon after Proctor arrived at Fort Franklin, the Seneca chief Cornplanter visited him.

Cornplanter (c.1732 - February 18, 1836)

The son of Dutch trader Johannes "John" Abeel II and Gah-hon-no-neh, a Seneca woman whose name means "She Who Goes to the River", Cornplanter was native to a Seneca village called Canawaugus. This village is now called Caledonia on the west side of the Genesee River in New York. His mother raised him in her tribe and his Seneca name was Gaiänt'wakê, which means "the planter." The Seneca used a matrilineal system of family relationships. His mother was a member of the influential Wolf Clan, thus Cornplanter occupied a position in that clan, which traditionally produced many of the Seneca's war chiefs.

Revolutionary War

The Iroquois Nation stayed neutral during the early stages of the Revolutionary War, however eventually the Six Nations did eventually join on the side of the British. Cornplanter and his tribe participated in the Battle of Wyoming Valley in 1778, which was a tragic defeat for the Americans. Other fierce battles followed which prompted General George Washington to send General John Sullivan on an expedition against the Iroquois in the summer of 1779. The general employed a "scorched earth" policy against the native, destroying villages, crop fields and food stores. The following winter many of the Iroquois died of cold and starvation. After the war, Cornplanter decided it was best to make peace with the Americans. He made the first of several trips to Philadelphia in 1790 to negotiate treaties with Pennsylvania, New York and the United States. These entities acquired thousands of acres of lands from the Seneca tribe during these negotiations. In early 1791, the government had granted Cornplanter 1,500 acres in Pennsylvania on the west bank of the Allegheny River. It was here that Cornplanter had established his village and tried to adopt European ways.

Many Meetings

During his time at Fort Franklin, Proctor negotiated at the fort and at the nearby French Creek Indian village. He stayed at Fort Franklin until departing for Buffalo Creek with his meeting with the Wabash River tribes on April 13.

April 13, 1791 - Proctor's Party Departs Fort Franklin for Buffalo Creek

Proctor's party set off from Fort Franklin, up the Allegheny River, bound for Buffalo Creek. On the fifteenth, Proctor became ill and traveled ahead to Cornplanter's village to receive treatment from a native doctor. His retinue caught up with him on April 17. The company remained in Cornplanter's Town for several days. While there, Proctor dispatched a letter to Secretary Knox and received word from Buffalo Creek that the various tribes had gathered and were awaiting him. The party departed from Cornplanter's Village on April 23, leaving the river and traveling overland. They arrived at Lake Erie on April 26 and completed their journey to Buffalo Creek on the 27th.

April 27, 1791 - Proctor's Party Arrives at Buffalo Creek

Proctor's party arrived at Buffalo Creek on April 27. The Seneca chief Red Jacked greeted him on his arrival.

Red Jacket (c. 1750–January 20, 1830)

Historians do not know the name of Red Jacket's father, but speculate that he was a member of the Cayuga tribe. His mother was named Ahweyneyonhn, or "Drooping Blue Flower". The place of Red Jacket's birth is also a matter of speculation. Many postulate that Geneva, Canoga, Ganundewah, or Canandaigua Lake was his birthplace, however Red Jacket maintained his mother gave birth to him near a sandbar on western branch of Lake Keuka, by Basswood Creek. A stone monument at this location marks the spot he said was his birthplace. His birth name was Otetiani, Always Ready. Because of the matrilineal kinship system the Iroquois used, Red Jacket was a member of his mother's clan, the Wolf Clan. During the Revolutionary War Red Jacket received his nickname because he wore a red jacket. He and his tribe sided with the British during the war, however after it ended, Red Jacket became known as a peacemaker and for his oratorical skills.

Buffalo Creek

Still under strong British influence from its proximity to the English strongholds Fort Niagara and Fort Erie, Buffalo was only about six miles from the latter and thirty-five miles from the former. The village had about 170 houses and the natives that inhabited this village were better fed and clothed than many of the other villages Proctor had visited on his journey.

Council

Upon their arrival, Red Jacket invited Proctor to attend a council in the council house. As they approached the structure, some of the natives fired a cannon that they had overloaded with powder in honor of Proctor's safe arrival. The force of the blast overturned both the gun and its carriage. Proctor entered the council house and announced to the assemblage that President Washington had sent him and truly represented the Thirteen Fires. Proctor warned them that if they continued their attacks, the United States would launch a devastating raid against them. He indicated that he wanted a delegation of warriors to accompany him up the Maumee River to hold a conference at Kekionga. A French fur trader in attendance rose to speak, telling Proctor that if he were to proceed along to Kekionga, he and all his companions would be killed. At length, they agreed to send a runner to Fort Erie to fetch the British commander of that post. After dealing with several other matters, the council adjourned until the next day.

May 23, 1791 - General Scott Begins March to Fort Ouiatenon

May 10 had come and gone. Scott had heard nothing about Thomas Proctor's mission and the violence had increased as time passed. Guessing that Proctor had failed, Scott departed Kentucky as he and his 750 men and officers forded the Ohio River near the Kentucky River's mouth in a heavy rain. Their destination lay 155 miles to the northwest through a heavily forested terrain interrupted only by streams, rivers and swamp. The troops entered the future state of Indiana near the current Switzerland and Jefferson County line. Their course would take them through Switzerland, Jefferson, Jennings, Scott, Bartholomew, Shelby, Johnson, Marion, Hendricks, Boone, Montgomery and Tippecanoe counties. Some of the troops would also travel through Warren and Fountain Counties. No American had traveled through this forest before. Scott used only the North Star to take his bearings as they traveled through this beautiful land, crossing rain-swollen rivers and streams. His course was almost in a straight line as he traversed along much of the watercourse of the White River. On June 1, Scott and his men reached the region near the fort.

May 15, 1791 - St. Clair Arrives Fort Washington

St. Clair had departed Washington DC on March 23, 1791, bound for Fort Washington. He had delayed his journey in Philadelphia due to illness. Even though his Quartermaster General Hogdon was in the city during the same time, apparently the two men did not confer. After St. Clair departed from Fort Pitt meetings with Kentucky militia units along the way further delayed his arrival at Fort Washington. When he did arrive on May 15, he had fewer than 100 troops ready for action. His Quartermaster General had not arrived, and would not arrive for months, so it fell to St. Clair to begin the arduous task of gathering supplies for an army that was supposed number 4000 men eventually. The army's scheduled departure date was July 10, 1791, less than two months away.

May 21, 1791 - Proctor Departs Buffalo

After weeks of travel and more weeks of deliberation, Proctor's mission had failed. The anger of the Shawnee and Miami of the Wabash River region prevented him from going into their lands to implore them forsake war. Additionally, he learned that British agents had gone into their territory not to make peace, but to agitate them and create more anger. The British kept the natives supplied with food and other supplies at their post at Fort Ouiatenon and Kekionga. Resigned to the defeat of his mission, Proctor departed Buffalo for Pittsburg, arriving there on June 6.

May 21, 1791 - John Van Cleve Shot at in his Fields

A band of Indian warriors hid in the forest near John Cleve's fields, watching him work, firing a shot at him as he worked early in the day on May 21.

Dangerous Times

The natives, especially the Shawnee, had become bold in their harassment of the settlers. Angered by the loss of their lands and emboldened by their victory over General Harmar in October 1790, they sometimes lurked in the fields and gardens around Fort Washington at night. Van Cleve had had some close encounters with warriors during this time. The settlers received news almost daily of attacks at nearby settlements on the Little Miami or the Great Miami. They heard the screams of a group of settlers captured at the mouth of Deer Creek as the natives tortured and killed within earshot of the town.

The Incident

Most settlers during this time of strife lived within the fort. They had their gardens and fields on out lots outside the fort, which they would work on during the daytime, returning in the evening to the fort's protection. On May 21,

John and another settler named Joseph Cutter worked their plots near each other when the shot rang out. A few minutes later, they fell upon Joseph Cutter and abducted him. John gave the alarm by hallowing (hollering). Each settler, as they worked, heard the yell and repeated it. Word in this way passed quickly to nearby settlements and a band of settlers soon appeared at the fort. The men began the search at the top of the hill on which he had been working. They found his shoe, which he had lost, and located the trail; however, after an extensive search they found nothing. After searching until nightfall, they returned to the fort. In the morning, they tried again, however the trail had gone cold. Cutter had disappeared from the settlement and from history.

May 22, 1791 - Major-General Richard Butler Arrives at Fort Pitt

Major-General Richard Butler arrived at Fort Pitt to begin recruiting soldiers and gathering supplies for General St. Clair's offensive against the Miami's at Kekionga.

Richard Butler (April 1, 1743 – November 4, 1791)

The son of Thomas and Eleanor Parker Butler, Richard was native to St. Bridget's Parish, Dublin, Ireland. The family migrated to Lancaster, Pennsylvania where Richard learned the gunsmith trade from his father who had opened a shop in the city. Richard learned the craft of building rifles and soon specialized in building the popular Pennsylvania long rifles. The family next moved Carlisle, Pennsylvania, where they continued to build the guns. Richard and his brother William moved to the Fort Pitt area where they became traders.

Revolutionary War

The Continental Congress appointed Butler as a commissioner to help negotiate with the Shawnee and Delaware tribes to support the American cause or remain neutral in it. In 1776, he received a commission as a major in the 8th Pennsylvania Regiment of the Continental Army. A year later, he gained command of the 9th Pennsylvania Regiment as a colonel. He and his regiment took part in the Battle of Saratoga and the Battle of Monmouth. He and his five brothers fought bravely during the war, drawing praise from General George Washington at its conclusion.

Post Revolution

After the War, Butler received an appointment to serve as Indian commissioner, during which time he negotiated the Treaty of Fort Stanwix in 1784. He later returned to Pennsylvania, where he became a judge. He married Maria Smith, with whom he had four children. Before his marriage to Maria, Butler had a relationship with the female Shawnee chief Nonhelema, who was also known as the "Grenadier Squaw." A son, Tamanatha Butler, was born from this relationship. In 1791, he Secretary of War Henry Knox granted Butler a commission as major general and second in command to General Arthur St. Clair.

June 1, 1791 - Destruction of Fort Ouiatenon

General Charles Scott located villages and the fort on June 1, 1791. They moved into the area, fought the Battle of the Kickapoo and burned the fort, villages and most of the crops.

Kickapoo

The Kickapoo name derives from the Algonquin work "Kiwegapawa," which means, "he stands about" or "he moves about." The tribe was closely allied with the Shawnee and their language was quite similar, as well as the Fox, Sauk, Mascouten tribes. The Kickapoo probably originated in northwest Ohio and southern Michigan in the area between Lake Erie and Lake Michigan. During the Beaver Wars (1642 - 1698), the Iroquois forced the tribe into southwest Wisconsin. About 1700 the tribe began the move into eastern Illinois. By 1791, the Kickapoo occupied areas in northern and eastern Illinois and western Indiana along the Wabash River. The tribe at this time numbered about 3,000 in this region. The Shawnee and the Kickapoo believed that the two tribes had the same origin that had divided over a dispute over a bear's claw. Like most of the Woodland tribes, the Kickapoo lived in fixed villages of longhouses during the summer months where they grew maize, squash, beans and other crops. In the fall after harvest, the tribe held its annual buffalo hunt and then the villagers separated to move into smaller hunting camps.

Nearing Ouiatenon

Scott and his force entered the beautiful lands near Ouiatenon, they lunched on a lovely stretch of prairie. After dining, one of the soldiers saw a solitary warrior seated on a horse, watching them. Scott and his force set off in immediate pursuit; however, the brave knew the country and had a fast horse, so he eluded them by riding along a ridge that divided the heavily forested land on either side.

Battle of Kickapoo

As the force entered a hilly area, they could see the vast expanse of the Wea Plains. At this point, Scott divided his force, sending Colonel John Harden to lead one part while he led the other. They sighted two Kickapoo villages, which the tribe had established as temporary camps while the hunted with the nearby Miami Indians, and quickly progressed towards them. The Kickapoo did not know of the presence of the American force until it was about a mile from their villages. The Indians quickly mounted their horses and set off for a ford of the Wabash that was the only safe, rocky-bottomed ford between the Vermillion and Tippecanoe Rivers. The ford was about eight miles from the villages. The natives made an immediate crossing of the ford, pursued by the American force. The Americans caught up with the Kickapoos at a spot about two miles north of the junction of Big Pine Creek and the Wabash, southeast of the current town of Independence in Warren County. The Americans defeated the natives, killing six and capturing fifty-two prisoners. They fought another skirmish with a band of warriors that had crossed the Wabash in canoes. The Americans killed several of these warriors. Scott's forces suffered only two wounded.

Destruction of the Fort

After his victory, Scott had Ouiatenon and its seventy buildings, many of which the natives had furnished quite well, and much corn. The troops also destroyed many other stores the natives needed to survive.

Decline

After its destruction, the area fell into decline, from which it never recovered. Though the remnants remained visible for many years, nature eventually reclaimed the site.

Reconstructed

Visitors may visit a replica of Fort Ouiatenon constructed by Dr. Richard B. Wetherill in 1930. Archeologists have located the actual site of the fort about a mile downstream. The National Register of Historic Places has listed the actual location of the fort in 1970. The eighteen-acre park is open on weekends from May through September.

Historic Fort Ouiatenon Park

3129 S River Rd

West Lafayette, IN 47906

(765) 476-8411

http://www.tcha.mus.in.us/ouiatenon.htm

June 02, 1791 - Scott Has Kethtipecanunck Destroyed

General Charles Scott, after his success at Ouiatenon, determined that he wanted to destroy the town of Kethtipecanunck, or Tippecanoe.

Kethtipecanunck or Tippecanoe

This village, established in the Eighteenth Century, had grown into an important trading center. It had a sizable population of French fur traders.

The Raid on Kethtipecanunck

Lieutenant Colonel James Wilkinson led the raid against the village with 360 men. Scott had wanted to send his entire force, however both men and horses were in poor condition. The soldiers departed in the early morning hours and reached the village about 4:30 in the afternoon. Wilkinson ordered an immediate attack, however most of the inhabitants had fled into the forests on his approach. After firing several shots, the soldiers pillaged the town, finding many books, letters and other documents that indicated that the inhabitants received a great deal of support from the British post at Detroit. They burned the village and as much of the corn and other food supplies that, they could find before returning to camp.

Scorching the Area

Scott, in Wilkinson's absence, had spent the time laying waste to all the native villages in the area he could find. Systematically, he had the villages pillaged and then burned. By the time Wilkinson returned, the native towns in the area were smoldering ruins.

June 04, 1791 - Scott Released Prisoners

Three days after his victory over the natives at Fort Ouiatenon, General Charles Scott released sixteen of the fifty-eight prisoners his troops had taken. These prisoners were the weakest and most infirm. He would turn the remaining forty-two over to Captain Joseph Ashton of the First United States regiment, at Fort Steuben at the Falls of the Ohio. After lamenting that he could not march to the head of the Wabash River because of the condition of his troops, he destroyed the villages around the fort along with their attendant gardens and returned to Kentucky.

June 14, 1791 - Scott Returns to Fort Finney

General Charles Scott brought his small army of 500 men back to Fort Finney at the Falls of the Ohio on June 14. His troops had suffered five wounded and no casualties. His troops had captured fifty-seven prisoners and killed thirty-eight warriors. The local citizens feted the returning troops with a generous banquet, provided a leading citizen of Louisville. The success of the mission lead a pleased Secretary of War Henry Knox to encourage Kentuckians to lead more similar missions into the region, which led Scott to organize two more missions. One, led by Colonel John Edwards and a second by his second in command on the June mission, Lieutenant Colonel James Wilkinson were sent out. Edwards' mission accomplished little; however, Wilkinson's was more successful.

June 13, 1791 - First Troops Arrive at Fort Washington for St. Clair's Campaign

The first troops recruited by General Richard Butler begin to arrive two months after his arrival at Fort Pitt.

Problems

Problems beset Butler's effort to recruit, supply and dispatch the troops needed for General St. Clair's campaign against the Miami at Kekionga. He lacked basic supplies the troops needed. Clothing, shoes, canteens, kettles, tents and field provisions were all in short supply. He also lacked the means to transport the troops from Fort Pitt to Fort Washington. On top of this, rainfall had been scanty and water levels in the Ohio River were insufficient to float the flatboats downriver to Fort Washington. Due to the low river levels, the voyage from Fort Pitt to Fort Washington took fifteen days.

Recruiting

Butler was to recruit 2,000 men with six-month enlistment periods. The operation was to commence on July 10, 1791, thus Butler worked in haste to recruit the soldiers, supply then and send them downriver. He organized them into small companies. Thus, sometime around May 29, he dispatched the first group of recruits downriver. Over the next three days, he sent several more flotillas of flatboats laden with men and supplies. Once they arrived, they would train with the regular troops already stationed at the fort.

June 25, 1791 - St. Clair Requests Kentucky Send another Expedition against Natives

Scott's expedition had gone so well that Secretary of War Knox suggested several times that St. Clair send out another. Finally, on June 25, 1791 St. Clair dispatched a letter to the Kentucky Board of War, requesting that they send another expedition into the Wabash region to raid. General Scott responded by commanding the second in command of his first mission, Lieutenant James Wilkinson to undertake preparation for another raid into Indian territory. The 500 troops were to muster at Fort Washington on July 15, and no later that the 20th, for a mission against Kenapacomaqua on the Wabash River.

July 30, 1791 - Captain Samuel Newman Departs Philadelphia

On September 4, 1791, Lieutenant Samuel Newman, commanding an eighty-man company belonging to the Second Regiment of Infantry, departed from Springfield, Massachusetts on July 30, 1791, bound for Fort Washington.

Samuel Newman (? - November 4, 1791)

Little is known about Samuel's early life other than that he had five brothers, all of whom enlisted in the same company. Five of the brothers died in the battle, only Robert survived and went on to be an author living in Virginia. Samuel served in the Revolutionary War as a lieutenant in Crafts' Artillery Regiment from May 1776 until December 1779. He later joined the Continental Navy, serving until the war ended. He became a member of the Society of the Cincinnati in 1784. He received appointment as a lieutenant of the 2nd U.S. Infantry Regiment on March 4, 1791.

Second Regiment of Infantry

Formed on March 3, 1791, the Second Regiment of Infantry was slated to consist of a lieutenant colonel commandant, two majors, eight captains, eight lieutenants, eight ensigns, one surgeon, two surgeon's mates, and eight companies of about 100 men each. Lieutenant Colonel James Wilkinson received appointment as commander of the regiment.

Departure

The company mustered and began their march at about 6:30 PM with eighty-one soldiers and four women on a dry, dusty day in August. The company also included five prisoners that had been arrested for desertion, one on suspicion of being a deserter and four men held prisoner for other crimes. The company camped at Follarny Hill, which is about three miles from Philadelphia, stopping at about 10:00 PM. The company would follow a road known as the e Old Glade Road. Later on, this road would be called the Pennsylvania Road and today approximates the course of the Pennsylvania Railroad. Newman's company also escorted several wagon loads of ordinance bound for Fort Washington.

Author's Note:

Captain Samuel Newman participated in St. Clair's Defeat and died in the battle. He left a journal of his experiences as commander of the company. The author used portions of his journal in this time line. Anyone interested in this journal can find it here:

http://content.wisconsinhistory.org/cdm/ref/collection/wmh/id/829

July 01, 1791 - Blacksmith John Van Cleve Killed and Scalped Outside Fort Washington

On June 31, a few days after a band of Indians shot at Van Cleve and abducted Joseph Cutter, several Indian warriors tried to abduct Van Cleve as he worked in his fields. Van Cleve, a strong man, managed to throw them off and escape. The next day as Van Cleve and two other men worked their crops a band of warriors tried to abduct them again. The three men took off running towards the fort. Van Cleve, a fast runner, passed the other two men. However, as he passed under a tree, an Indian who had been waiting in ambush, jumped down on top of him. Again, Van Cleve threw off his attacker. But the man had a knife with which he stabbed Van Cleve, killing him. The warrior scalped him and fled. After the incident, the settlers found his body. The warrior had stabbed him five times. Benjamin Van Cleve, John's son, led a posse that searched out the natives and attacked them near a creek. A settler named Samuel Thompson managed to cut off the hand of the Indian that killed Van Cleve.

Dayton

Catherine, John's wife, now had two young children and no father. She married Samuel Thomson and the couple had two more children. They later migrated to settle into newly founded Dayton, Ohio.

July 10, 1791 - Scheduled Departure of St. Clair's Army

General Arthur St. Clair had intended to begin his campaign against the tribes assembled at Kekionga. However, the multitude of problems kept the army in camp. Recruiting and supply problems were the biggest causes for the delay. Most of the force he intended to use on the campaign was still en route to Fort Washington. His quartermaster general Samuel Hodgdon was still in Pennsylvania and would not arrive until early September. St. Clair's army would not depart until mid-September, allowing the natives to gather more reinforcements from faraway tribes. Some historians that have studied the campaign believe that if St. Clair could have left at the time he desired those other tribes would not have had time to assemble. As it was, in addition to the Miami, the Ottawa, Chippewa, Pottawatomie and other tribes had sufficient time to move into the area and oppose St. Clair's army.

August 01, 1791- Lieutenant Colonel James Wilkinson Departs Fort Washington to Raid

Colonel James Wilkinson led an attack into the Northwest Territory against the Miami town of Kenapacomaqua, located on the Eel River about six miles north of the present town of Logansport, Indiana. Wilkinson departed Fort Washington with about 500 mounted Kentucky militiamen.

James Wilkinson (March 24, 1757 – December 28, 1825)

The son of Joseph Wilkinson and Alethea Heighe Wilkinson, James was native to Benedict, Maryland. Wilkinson enrolled in the University of Pennsylvania to study medicine, but the Revolutionary War interrupted his studies. He joined the Continental Army, serving until 1781, when he resigned. He later served in the Pennsylvania militia and moved to Kentucky in 1784, where he helped gain statehood for Kentucky. He received his commission as Colonel in the United States Army in 1791.

August 01, 1791 - St. Clair's Army Camps Ludlow Station

The soldiers billeted at Fort Washington, on the Ohio River, had found the fort a good source of liquor and other debaucheries. In order to keep the soldiers away from such temptations, St. Clair ordered the army to move five miles inland, to Ludlow Station on Mill Creek. In addition to this, he expected the site would prove to have better pasturage for the horses.

August 04, 1791 - Newman's Company Camps at Lancaster

By August 4, Newman's company had made it as far as Lancaster, Pennsylvania. Progress had been slow, as the soldiers were not used to marching and Newman had to make camp early on the August 1.

The March

Newman had been ordered by Secretary Knox to accept into the march a woman named Mary Hastings, whom he termed a "bitch" and swore he would "drum her out," at first opportunity. Women and children of various sorts and ages had been allowed to accompany St. Clair's force as they moved. There were as many as 200 of these "camp followers," accompanied the army when it went into battle. The vast majority of these women and children died in the aftermath of the disaster. Captain Newman had posted a squad of guards at the rear of the column to prevent deserters; however, on the night of August 4 two men deserted during their watches. He had problems with many of the men getting drunk and on August 2 had had four men flogged for becoming severely drunk and disorderly. Newman had to berate the soldiers often in order to make them keep themselves clean as well as clean their weapons and keep them in good repair. Most mornings the company started the march between 4:00 and 5:00 AM. While camped at Lancaster, Newman ordered the men to wear their dress blue uniforms. Many of the men at this point were lame and quite fatigued by the pace of the march. He allowed the company to remain in camp until Monday to rest and heal.

August 07, 1791 - Battle of Kenapacomaqua

Kenapacomaqua

The village Kenapacomaqua was scattered along a three-mile length on the north bank of the Eel River north of its junction with the Wabash River. The uneven boggy terrain, mostly covered with scrub oak, plum, black jack, bramble and hazel thickets, proved difficult for the army to navigate. Besides Kenapacomaqua , the town had many other names, including Kikiah, Kenapeco-maqua Town, Eel River Town, L'Anguille, Snakefish Town, The Snakelike Fish, Eel Town and "ye olde village," or Olde Towne.

The Battle

Wilkinson had moved his force of 523 soldiers had departed Fort Washington, present day Cincinnati, on August 1, 1791. Moving through the densely forested terrain in current southeastern Indiana, Wilkinson's soldiers arrived at the town during the afternoon of August 7 and launched an immediate attack on the Miami village. The American force killed nine natives, including six warriors, two women and one child. Two soldiers died in the battle. Wilkinson's men captured thirty-four prisoners, one of which was Miami Chief Little Turtle's daughter. They also released one white captive. After the battle, Wilkinson burned the corn and other crops in the area.

Cemetery

Some years after the battle, some of the soldiers that fought in it returned to the area and identified the place they had buried the two soldiers that died. The cemetery contains the remains of John Bartlett and an unknown soldier. Located near the junction of Mud Creek and the Eel River along County Road 250 North, the cemetery has marble memorial stones marking the approximate location of the remains. The exact location will never be known, as the army took steps to disguise the grave's location by burning huge bonfires over the spot to keep the natives from disinterring and desecrating the bodies.

August 09, 1791 - Wilkinson Destroys Kethtipecanunck

After the Battle of Kenapacomaqua Wilkinson decided, he wanted to strike at the main Kickapoo town known as "in the prairie."

"In The Prairie."

The town Wilkinson knew was on the main Potawatomi trail that traveled south from Lake Michigan. Wilkinson had faulty knowledge of the location of this town. He thought it was on the Illinois River in present day Indiana. In reality, the village he sought was on Big Pine creek, about two miles west present-day Oxford in Benton County, Indiana at a place known as Indian Hill. It was about twenty miles from current day Lafayette. The Potawatomi trail began at Blue Island in Chicago and traveled first west into current Illinois, then back through Benton County Indiana crossing Big Pine Creek and ending at Lafayette. It was an important fur-trading route used by the natives and fur traders.

Flailing About

Wilkinson would never approach this town, as his troops became entangled in the swampy prairie and spent a long, frustrating day flailing about in the difficult terrain. At the end of the day, they had traveled about thirty miles. He managed to get back on the Tippecanoe Trail where his exhausted men and horses camped at around seven o'clock in the evening. At around four in the morning on August 9, Wilkinson and his small army once again started out, discovering the Indian village of Kethtipecanunck, which Scott had visited in June. Scott had destroyed the cornfields, however the natives had re-planted the corn and it was growing well. Wilkinson destroyed it, and, the natives having fled as he approached, began again his quest of finding the Kickapoo town.

August 11, 1791 - Newman's Company Stops Due to Heavy Rain

During the pause, Newman had distributed the soldier's pay on Saturday, which the paymaster had given him before the troops left Philadelphia. He regretted it, as it just gave the soldiers money to buy more rum. The company commenced marching at 4:00 AM on Monday. By August 11, Newman's company had marched about forty-two miles from Lancaster, crossing Swatara Creek, which was knee deep. On August 9, Newman had ejected one of the women, Mrs. Graham, for bringing canteens filled with rum on three occasions during the morning. He had warned her repeatedly and finally tossed her out and hoped the example he set for her would teach the other women on the march a lesson. On August 10, a Wednesday, the troops crossed the Susquehanna River and camped at Silver Springs. Three days of rain and river crossings had soaked the men and most of the supplies, so Captain Newman delayed the days march until 2:00 PM, when the company resumed the march. The road was muddy from the incessant thunderstorms.

August 12, 1791 - Wilkinson Begins Return

Wilkinson's desire to destroy the Kickapoo town did not materialize. He and his men managed to destroy more crops in the villages along the Wabash; however, the protests of his troops forced him to reconsider. On August 12, 1791, Wilkinson found the road that Scott's troops had cut through the forest on their return to Fort Finney. Scott and his force entered this road and returned to the Ohio River, completing a successful mission deep into Indian country.

August 14, 1791 - Captain Newman Reclaims Two Prisoners at Chambersburg

The march from Silver Springs to Carlisle had been eventful. He had thrown two women from the camp on Friday, August 12. Mrs. Willingham had repeatedly brought rum into the camp, so he had her removed. He had punished Robert Cook with twenty-eight lashes and John Peters twenty for getting drunk. During the punishment Mrs. Brady had provoked Captain Newman with her insolent language and behavior, so he had her ejected. He had ordered the women's provisions be given to some of the other soldier's wives who had behaved tolerably. He lamented the large number of women that accompanied the troops and the poor quality of the conscripts that comprised the content of his troops.

Reprieve

On Saturday, August 13, Mrs. Brady had snuck back into camp. She implored the captain to allow her to stay, as she would not be able to carry her infant child with her in addition to all her clothing on the 120-mile march back to Philadelphia. On her promise of good behavior, the captain allowed her to stay. Newman's problems with deserters continued, as he had almost as many prisoners as he did guards.

Sore Feet and Deserters

On Sunday, the Captain awoke to a lame foot, which was sore, and enflamed, making the march difficult. The company commenced marching at 4:00 AM on a fine morning. During the march, he received word of two men held prisoner at Chambersburg. The company reached a nice stream near Shippensburg where they camped. He sent a sergeant and four men to retrieve the deserters. He sent a letter along that gave the jailers vouchers that included a ten-dollar bounty plus jailing expenses for the men. In the letter, he excoriated the deserters, calling them villains for stealing bounty money, clothing and sustenance from the country and then abandoning their comrades. At four o'clock AM the next morning, the company resumed the march.

August 17, 1791- Provision Wagon Breaks Down - Captain Newman's Journal

Drunken and deserting soldiers had plagued Captain Newman since the march began on July 30. Further compounding his frustration, on August 17 the provision wagon containing the tents and Newman's baggage had broken down. The bad roads and rainy weather had made it impossible for the wagons to keep up with the main body of the troops. Shortly after receiving this bad new, the rain began again. Since the day's march was almost over, Newman found a horse barn along the road that had straw in it. He had the men bed down in the straw. Further, the men forming the rear guard had gotten drunk and allowed one of the prisoners to slip out of his shackles and escape.

August 19, 1791 - The March Continues - Captain Newman's Journal

The soldiers camped under the horse shed through the night of August 17. The rain began again, turning the ground wet, making a disagreeable campsite. The wagons that had broken down came into camp about 9:00 in the morning. Newman decided to stay camped in the horse shed until the weather cleared, rather than setting up the tents in the rain. He discovered a plot, planned by a sentry that stood watch over the deserters kept chained at the rear of the camp. The sentry had conspired to help the prisoners escape and then he would desert with them. Newman had the sentry tied to a wagon wheel and given fifty hard lashes, and then confined with the other prisoners. He would have the lot face court martial when they arrived at Fort Pitt. Another incident occurred in which a rattlesnake bit one of the sergeants. The man was wearing loose overalls, so the snake's fangs did not sink into flesh. They killed the snake. On the morning of August 19, the weather was still cloudy and windy. Newman had the men roused at 6:00 AM and by 7:00; they resumed the march to Fort Pitt.

August 27, 1791 - Newman's Company Arrives at Fort Pitt - Captain Newman's Journal

The march over the next few days proved largely uneventful. Newman had some deserters punished and chained and drew provisions and complained of the condition of the roads the company traversed. Heavy rain and thunderstorms inundated the men several times, muddying roads and increasing the difficulty of the march. Finally, at around 11:00 AM on August 27, Newman's company reached Fort Pitt. Newman's company set up camp and prepared for the next leg of the journey, the flatboat ride down the Ohio River to Fort Washington.

September 05, 1791 - Captain Samuel Newman Departs Fort Pitt

Newman's company had stayed in camp at Fort Pitt eight days waiting for the Ohio River levels to rise enough for the troops to enter the barges constructed to transport them to Fort Washington.

Fort Pitt

Fort Pitt was the third fortress constructed on the site. George Washington had first seen the Forks of the Ohio, the site of the fort's location, on November 24, 1753 while on a mission to Fort Le Boeuf on Lake Erie for British Governor Robert Dinwiddie. On Washington's advice, Dinwiddie had sent a company of men commanded by Captain William Trent to construct a fort. Trent and his men had arrived at the site and began construction of a fort Trent would call it Fort George, for the Prince of Wales George, who would become King George III in 1760.

The French Capture Fort George

A French military strike drove Trent and his men from the site before he could finish it. The French tore down the British fort and constructed a new one beginning on April 17, 1754, that they would call Fort Duquesne.

The British Capture Fort Duquesne

The French held the site until November 24, 1758, when the French commander had the fort burned to prevent its capture by the British during General John Forbes campaign. George Washington and his troops occupied the site the next day. During the campaign to capture the fort, General Forbes had been sick, so British General John Stanwix took over construction of the new fort, which he would name Fort Pitt, after British Prime Minster William Pitt. The British abandoned the fort in 1772, sold it and turned it over to the jurisdiction of the Province of Pennsylvania.

Fort Dunmore

Virginia claimed the fort in 1774 and Virginia Governor Lord Dunmore sent Dr. John Connolly to raise a militia and take command of the fort. Connolly traveled to the Forks of the Ohio, began recruiting a force, and renamed it Fort Dunmore. Dunmore ordered that area residents begin paying Virginia taxes later that year. In May 1775, frontiersmen in the region met at Pittsburg, voted to support their counterparts in Massachusetts. Connolly outnumbered and in hostile territory, abandoned the fort.

Fort Pitt Once Again

On August 7, 1775 Captain John Neville, along with a force of about 100 men, reoccupied the fort and renamed it Fort Pitt. The Americans used the fort as a base of operations during the Revolutionary War; however, no action took place there. The Commonwealth of Pennsylvania took possession of the fort after the war ended. During the Northwest Indian War, Major Isaac Craig had the fort repaired in 1791. The Army decommissioned the fort on August 3, 1797.

John Neville (July 26, 1731 - July 29, 1803)

The son of Joe Neville and Ann Bohannan Neville, John was native to Abington Parrish, Gloucester, Province of Virginia. In 1754, he and Winifred Oldham married. The couple would have three children. Neville served under Lieutenant Colonel George Washington during the Battle of Jimonville Glen and with General Edward Braddock. After Braddock's campaign to capture Fort Duquesne failed, Neville returned to Winchester, Virginia to serve as a Justice of the peace and sheriff of Frederick County, and Vestryman of the Episcopal Church. During the border dispute with Pennsylvania, Virginia sent Captain John Neville and 100 Virginia militiamen to occupy the fort after Connolly had fled.

Waiting for the River to Rise

In spite of the rain Newman's company had been subjected to, Ohio River levels had been low, preventing the flow of men and supplies downriver to the delayed St. Clair campaign. Somewhere in the neighborhood of 100 barges had been built to carry these men and supplies downriver. Newman's men spent the time healing themselves from the hurts of the long march. Heavy rains ensued on September 3, bringing river levels up. Newman began gathering provisions for his men. On September 5, levels had risen high enough for his men to enter the barges and begin the 600-mile journey downriver to Fort Washington.

September 06, 1791 - Soldiers Begin Cutting Road Through the Forest

On September 5, 1791, a small contingent of soldiers began cutting a road, more accurately a rough path, through the wilderness to the site of the proposed construction site of Fort Hamilton. Fort Hamilton would be the first of a chain of forts St. Clair would have built to guard the army's supply line and provide a line of defense. The soldiers would take three days to build the road, a distance of about twenty miles.

September 07, 1791 - Newman's Company Arrives Muskingum Island

The Ohio River had risen with the recent rains, driving the flotilla of barges carrying men and supplies toward Fort Washington. Captain Newman's men occupied two of the barges. Newman assigned six watches and ordered the officer in charge of the second barge to do likewise and to stay within hailing distance. They encountered heavy rain on the afternoon they departed, which made everything and every one wet and uncomfortable. By 6:00 AM on the Sixth, the barges passed Buffalo Creek, on the banks of current day Wellsburg, West Virginia. They had now gone about seventy-two miles from Fort Pitt. Here, Newman sent one of the men ashore to get milk from the settlement there. On the morning of September 7, the watch sighted through his telescope a party of men filing through the bushes near the river's bank. Newman suspected these men were preparing to attack them, so he had his men prepare their weapons in anticipation. He kept them ready until the barges passed Muskingum Island, which lies in the middle of the river just past Marietta, Ohio. They passed this island about 3:00 PM on September 7. The barges stopped at this point, about 170 miles from Fort Pitt, to renew acquaintances with some men stationed on the blockhouse that stood on the island. They departed around 6:00 PM, accompanied by a party of men who gave Newman some squashes and watermelons. The men danced with some of the women on board until about 3:00 AM before rowing back to the island. At this point, the river current had grown quite strong, about 4.5 knots.

September 07, 1791 - Quartermaster General Samuel Hodgdon Arrives Fort Washington

Quartermaster General Samuel Hodgdon finally arrived at Fort Washington on the same day that Captain Samuel Newman's company arrived at the fort. Unfortunately, for the army the Quartermaster in charge of supplying their needs was both inexperienced in the needs of a frontier army and faithful in his promise to be economical in his procurement of supplies. Horses and many of the supplies were in short supply, of poor quality with most coming from western Pennsylvania using the long trip down the Ohio River as a supply line, not Kentucky, which was closer.

The Horses

Hodgdon had procured about 400 horses from Western Pennsylvania. Their condition deteriorated during the long trip downriver, as the men, transporting them did not have the means to care for them properly. By the time they arrived at Fort Washington, they were hungry and weak from the transport. As the season advanced past the originally scheduled mid-July departure date, forage for them around the fort diminished. Furthermore, he had not supplied hobbles or bells for the horses. Without them, the horses would wander into the forest and be lost or stolen by the natives that always lurked in the forests around the fort. Soldiers made hobbles from scraps of leather bridles. They kept the blacksmiths busy making bells, until they exhausted their supply of brass.

Other Supplies

Hodgson had purchased saddles for the horses; however, they were too large for the animals and thus did not fit properly. He had supplied only one grindstone for sharpening axes for a force that had to cut trees with axes to clear a road through the wilderness. Additionally, he had purchased only about one hundred poor quality axes for the soldiers to use. Leather splints that he had supplied were useless; thus, the soldiers had to make splints for injured soldiers on site using whatever materials they had. Contractors employed by Hodgson were mainly from Philadelphia and had most of their contacts in that area. Even though the settlements in Kentucky, some of which had been settled for nearly twenty years, could have supplied most of the army's needs, these contractors made little attempt to develop contacts there, leaving the long, difficult trip down the Ohio River as the army's tenuous supply line. Many of the supplies he purchased were surplus stock remaining from the Revolutionary War, and thus old and in poor condition. Beef was the meat of choice for the army. The army could purchase cattle to feed the troops, which could then walk along with the army. The soldiers slaughtered the cattle on site as needed.

The Road

The road cut by the soldiers was at best only a rough trail impassable by wagons filled with supplies. The contractors Hodgson employed to supply the army did not arrange to move supplies by boat, thus all supplies had to move by horseback. The horses, in poor condition due to lack of forage and inadequate care became so weakened, they could not carry full loads of supplies. All of these factors played an important role in the disaster that befell St. Clair's army in early November.

September 10, 1791 - Construction Begins on Fort Hamilton

Lieutenant Colonel William Darke and an advance party of soldiers arrived on the east bank of the Great Miami River on September 10, 1791 to pick a site on which to construct the first fort in the line of fortresses St. Clair would establish to guard his supply line.

William Darke (May 6, 1736 - November 26, 1801)

The son of Joseph Darke, William is native to Philadelphia County, Pennsylvania. Historians do not know the name of his mother. The family moved to Shepherdstown Virginia (now Berkley County, West Virginia) in 1740. His early history is murky; however, he did enlist in the militia during the early stages of the French and Indian War in 1755. Family tradition places him in the ranks that served under General Edward Braddock; however, historians do not. In 1766, he married a widow, Sarah Deleyea, whose maiden name is unknown. The couple had four children.

Revolutionary War

On February 9, 1776, Darke received a commission as captain of the 8th Virginia Regiment, a regiment that he recruited for service in the Continental Army. He gained promotion to major on January 4, 1777. During the October 4, 1777, the British captured him after he received a wound during the battle. He remained a prisoner on Long Island in New York for two years until released as part of a prisoner exchange. In early 1781, he gained promotion to lieutenant colonel, a rank he held for the remainder of the war. After General Lord Cornwallis surrendered on October 19, 1781 Darke remained in the army until 1783, when he retired.

Return to Berkeley County

After his retirement, he returned to Berkley County. The federal government granted him 6,666 2/3 acres as payment for his military service the year he retired. He received another 1111½ acres in 1780. In 1788, the voters of Berkley County elected him to serve on the Virginia convention that would decide the fate of the new United States Constitution. He voted to ratify the document. His next foray into politics came in 1791 when voters chose him to serve in the Virginia House of Delegates. However, President George Washington asked him to serve as lieutenant colonel in St. Clair's army, so he never took the seat in the House of Delegates.

Choosing the Site for Fort Hamilton

Darke chose a site on the east bank of the Great Miami River. An Indian path on both sides led to a river ford at the site. St. Clair had determined that the log stockade fort would serve as a supply depot for his troops; however, the steep drop of the river and resulting heavy current made it difficult for flatboats to ascend to the river to the fort. An attempt to move a shipment of 120 barrels of flour on September 17 failed.

September 11, 1791 - Newman's Company Arrives at Fort Washington

The morning of September 11 found Captain Newman's company within fourteen miles of Fort Washington. Captain Newman ordered the men to prepare themselves to look impressive when the flatboat landed. The boat stopped briefly at a settlement called Little Miami. Newman remarked on how beautiful the location was and that the people there appeared to be hard working and content. The flatboat then continued on, landing at Fort Washington at around 4:30 in the afternoon. General St. Clair greeted them and then Newman had the company set up camp in front of the fort.

September 15, 1791 - Newman's Company Departs for Fort Hamilton

During the intervening days, Newman wrote a report about the march and dined with General Harmar and some other officers. He and his men hauled the boats ashore on the thirteenth and found that someone had stolen twenty-five pounds of bacon from their stores. They managed to find the culprits, recover their bacon and punished them. On the fourteenth, the company busied themselves preparing for the march.

Beginning the March

They began the twenty-four mile march at eight o'clock in the morning under a drizzling rain. The road, muddy with rain, delayed the wagons hauling their baggage. They covered the ten-mile distance to Ludlow Station with difficulty, fording two streams and progressing slowly. Upon arrival at the camp at Ludlow station, they set up camp on a wet piece of ground. They slept without blankets in a dense fog that was so heavy that, even with fires, moistened their feet and clothing with its cold dampness. About midnight a large tree fell into the camp, killing one soldier and hurting another. The stricken man took three hours to die.

September 17, 1791 - St. Clair's Army Departs Ludlow Station

General Arthur St. Clair and his army set out from their camp at Ludlow Station on September 17, 1791. His force, at its peak, had totaled almost 2000 soldiers. However, many soldiers deserted their posts during their time at Ludlow Station. By the time they left on the 17, the force had dropped to about 1486 soldiers and around 250 camp followers. The camp followers consisted mostly of women that served as laundresses and prostitutes. A large number of children were also in the camp follower contingent.

September 17, 1791 - Newman's Company Arrive Fort Hamilton

Captain Samuel Newman's company took two days to march the thirty miles from Ludlow Station to Fort Hamilton on the banks of the Miami River. Progress was slow because the surveyors had not completely blazed the trail and Newman's company had to make a new road. The new road was somewhat longer than the original one, which was twenty-four miles. On the Seventeenth, the company commenced marching about 6:00 AM and arrived at Fort Hamilton around noon. The fort at this point had four companies of regular United States Troops, two battalions of levied troops and five pieces of artillery.

September 19, 1791 - Newman's Men Kill Rattlesnakes in Camp

Captain Newman records in his journal that the army had been ordered to stand at arms on September 17, from reveille until the morning fog cleared so the soldiers might discover any enemy that crept within 200 yards or so. The order required the men to remain on the parade ground for about two hours each day.

Fired Upon

He reports that a detachment of men sent out to guard a supply train returned to camp, relaying the news that the natives had fired on them numerous times, without effect. They had returned fire, also without effect. They had recovered a stolen horse, but had not seen any warriors, not even the ones that fired on them, having concealed themselves well in the surrounding forest.

Rattlesnakes and Thunderstorms

On the 19th Newman's men killed several large rattlesnakes in their camp. Someone reported seeing a band of ten Indians a short distance from camp and a detachment of men had been ordered out to find them. The patrol returned to camp and reported that the Indians were nowhere to be found. During the night, thunderstorms rolled in with fierce lightning, heavy rain and loud thunder. Newman reports that his tent was "tolerable," and he was able to use some of the tall, native grass as straw inside the tent, so he was reasonably comfortable.

September 21, 1791 - St. Clair Receives Information from Vincennes

The commander of the post at Vincennes' Fort Knox, Lieutenant Abner Prior, had obtained intelligence that the Indians gathered around Kekionga numbered about 1500 warriors. These warriors were eager for battle. He had sent this information on to St. Clair, who received the letter on September 21.

The Warriors

Little Turtle, the Miami chief that commanded the Indian's force, had divided the 1500 warriors of the chiefs that had decided to cooperate with him into groups of about twenty men. Four men in each group acted as hunters and gatherers for their group with the expectation that they would provide their companions with the food they obtained by noon each day. The approximately 280 hunters gathered about 200 deer and wild turkey in addition to small game like squirrels, rabbits and other wild animals. The warriors included elements from the Miami, Shawnee, Delaware, Wyandot, Ottawa, Chippewa and other tribes. Little Turtle had sent these small groups out into the countryside to keep watch on St. Clair's army as it moved. These scouting bands took turns observing the Americans, returning to Kekionga periodically and replaced by another. In this way, Little Turtle received periodic updates on St. Clair's movements. St. Clair was unaware that Little Turtle was keeping close watch on his force as it moved.

Insufficient Supplies

St. Clair's army, in contrast, suffered from inadequate supplies, shabby clothes, leaky tents, and poor quality shoes that seldom lasted a week under the rough conditions. There were not enough horses, and those the army had were too small and underfed, to transport the supplies along the uncertain road. Cincinnati was a new settlement and did not have the craftsmen necessary to maintain a nearby military force. St. Clair's men needed carpenters, coopers to make barrels, wheelwrights to repair wagon wheels, gunsmiths, blacksmiths and many other artisans with the skills necessary to a large military force. These men did not exist in proper quantity in or near the new settlement. Many also questioned the quality of the gunpowder, as it was leftover from the American Revolution. Many of the men reported that the powder misfired when they tried to use it. Since the powder had been improperly packed and then stored in tents that leaked when it rained, the powder could have been good, originally, but became defective due to improper storage during the campaign.

September 26, 1791 - Four of Newman's Men Desert

Newman reports that the next three days it rained, sometimes in torrents. His baggage still had not reached him and fretted that when they started marching, the increasing distance from Fort Washington would make it more difficult to get them. He also lamented the fact that soon autumn frosts would destroy the forage upon which the cattle and horses required to eat. The coming winter campaign in the poor quality tents and ban on having fires during a campaign created a great deal os anguish.

Deserters

On September 26, the sun returned. Newman took his tent down and allowed the ground under it to dry out. He also learned that four of his men had deserted. They had gotten permission to go to the river to wash. When they did not return, he learned they had left their dirty clothing behind and taken their best with them. He could only conclude that they had deserted, a common and potentially calamitous problem for St. Clair's entire army.

September 28, 1791 - Two of Newman's Men Disappear

Two of Captain Samuel Newman's men, a pair of brothers with the last name of Depwew, disappeared after Newman gave them permission to go to the river and wash up. It had been a thick fog enveloping the land during the morning hours and Newman feared that Indians had crept up on them and took them.

The same day, Newman served as President of a regimental Court-Martial.

September 29, 1791 - Brothers Depew Turn Up

Captain Samuel Newman received news that the brothers Depew had become lost in the forest and straggled into Dunlap's station. The commanding officer of the station was holding them on charges of desertion.

September 30, 1791 - Captain Newman's Men Help Finish Fort Hamilton

Captain Newman's company, along with a company of about 250 men, completed building the picket holes and cut slabs of wood to line it as well as the banqueting around it.

Basic Fort Construction

Typically, a fort of the type at Fort Hamilton consisted of wooden palisades, which consisted of logs anchored in a shallow ditch dug to support them. They slanted the logs slightly forward to create an obstacle to attackers. The soldiers sharpened the tops of the logs with axes. They used small to medium sized trees and left no space in between the logs to form a wall about ten to twelve feet high. Many times commanders took the additional step of lining the inside of the palisade wall with boards as a further defensive measure.

Picket Holes

The soldiers dug picket holes, or foxholes, in strategic spots around the fort. These were generally about four feet in diameter and about three feet deep. They usually piled the dirt removed from the pit in front as a parapet to protect the defender in the pit. Sometimes they made the pits larger to accommodate three for four men firing teams. These pits would have been between 50 to 300 yards from the wall and about 15 feet apart. Sometimes a trench connected the pits and a fire pit, or mess hole, dug to provide a place to build a fire and cook.

Banquette

The banquette, also called a firing step, was a wooden or earthen shelf built inside the walls of the stockade that allowed soldiers to step up over the palisade to fire at an attacker and then duck back down behind the wall.

Fort Hamilton

The fort was located along the Great Miami River and used the river as one side for protection. The size of the fort is unknown, however historians think it may have been the size of up to two football fields. A powder magazine was dug into the south wall. It included barracks for the soldiers, officer's quarters, granary, stables, kitchen, storehouse and cistern. The fort's primary purpose was to provide a storehouse and staging point for soldiers and supplies moving into the frontier. The State of Ohio has established a memorial on the site of Fort Hamilton that includes a model of the fort.

Fort Hamilton Memorial

One South Monument Ave

Hamilton, Ohio 45011

(513)867-5823

http://www.butlercountyohio.org/monument/index.cfm?page=fthamilton

October 01, 1791 - Warriors Kill Men and Steal Horses near Fort

The rain returned around 8:00 in the morning as Captain Newman and his men camped near Fort Hamilton. It rained all day and into the night. News trickled into the camp about small incidents near the fort. The roving bands of warriors kept a close watch upon the army, striking occasionally to abduct or kill soldiers and steal horses. They killed a man of the first regiment on this day and stole six horses about two miles from the camp. The officers ordered a group of men out to pursue the raiders. Another bit of news involved that a Major Davidson had been killed near the Great Miami River.

October 04, 1791 - St. Clair's Army Departs Fort Hamilton

General Arthur St. Clair and his army set out from Fort Hamilton for Kekionga at about 11:00 AM the morning of October 4, 1791. The army consisted of approximately 600 regular army troops, 800 six-month conscripts and 600 militia, totaling nearly 2000 troops. The force also included about 250 camp followers. They forded the Great Miami River, which was waist deep with a heavy current. The day was rainy, cold and damp, thus by the time they crossed the river the soldiers were wet, cold and uncomfortable.

Marching Order

Because of the narrowness and difficulty of the fresh cut road, the army marched in two columns, single file and spaced about two or three hundred yards apart. The cattle that served as food for the army and the horses occupied the space between the columns. Two pieces of artillery led and followed each column.

Camp

Two miles after crossing the river, the army stopped to make camp in a forest thick with brush and briars. They made warm fires and dried themselves by its heat. The soldier's camp formed an oblong square with each column maintaining its own camp the same distance apart as the columns had been.

October 13, 1791 - Captain Newman's Company Arrives at Site of Fort Jefferson

After a hard march over rough, freshly cleared road, Captain Newman, his company and the bulk of St. Clair's army arrived at the site of Fort Jefferson. During the march, much of which occurred during rainy, cold weather, the army was not allowed to light a fire at night for fear of the smoke revealing the army's position. They were not allowed to shoot at any wildlife they encountered for the same reason. Along the way, they had one or two encounters with parties of Indians. The soldiers shot at one, but missed.

Slow Progress

Progress was slow, as the soldiers had to cut the road through the forest as the traveled. The longest distance recorded in Captain Newman's journal is 7 1/2 miles and the shortest is three. On October 12, a band of scouts came across an Indian camp with a freshly slaughtered bear carcass and a deer on the fire cooking. The scouts took the meat and some animal skins back to the army. Newman writes of eating venison and bear meat that evening. On the same day, the soldiers discovered a party of Indians near the camp, which they fired on, wounding one. On October 13, the army moved about 6 1/2 miles, cutting the road as they went. At this point, they had traveled about 44 miles from Fort Hamilton. However, St. Clair ordered them back to their previous night's camp. The officers had decided to build a blockhouse and fort at a site near a spring that occupied a low knoll and had a good spring nearby.

October 14 1791 - Construction Begins on Fort Jefferson

The soldiers began the work of clearing the site the fort would occupy of trees. What should have been quick work turned out to be slow, as the quartermaster had not acquired enough axes. The soldiers only had about 200 axes, thus the remaining 1800 men had nothing to work with. Clearing the ground and building the fort would take ten days.

The state of Ohio has placed a memorial marker at the site of Fort Jefferson.

Fort Jefferson Memorial Park

3981 Weavers-Fort Jefferson Rd.

Greenville, OH 45331

https://www.ohiohistory.org/visit/museum-and-site-locator/fort-jefferson-park

October 18, 1791 - Six Men Desert - 60 Horse Convoy of Supplies Arrive

On October 18, a packhorse convoy of sixty horses arrived at the slowly rising Fort Jefferson. Most of these horses carried food, thus alleviating the shortage among the troops. However, the food was not nearly enough to last the remainder of the campaign. The cattle would last the army about three weeks and the flour only about four days. Six men disappeared from the camp the same day, probably deserters reacting to the lack of food, leaking tents and general despair that began to affect the entire camp. The Indians had kept close contact with the army and on occasion would strike, killing or abducting one or two soldiers or stealing horses or supplies.

Captain Newman's Journal

Newman relates that a Captain Shaylor had arrived from Fort Hamilton where he had been recovering from an illness. He reported that there were few supplies available to transport to the troops camped at Fort Jefferson. Newman noted that the forage for the horses had disappeared with the fall frosts and that some of them die of starvation every day. The heavy rains had left the already primitive road constructed by the troops almost impassable. The dire situation of the army created an attitude among the troops that encouraged desertion.

The seriousness of the situation caused General St. Clair to call a staff meeting the next day.

October 19, 1791 - General St. Clair Holds Staff Meeting

The lack of rations for the army caused General St. Clair much concern, so to deal with the problem he held a staff meeting on the morning of October 19. In the staff meeting, he issued the following orders:

The quartermaster officer of each regiment was to turn their packhorses over the contractor in charge of procuring supplies

The contractor was to add his own horses to the herd, go to Fort Washington and bring all of the supplies there

The third order put all troops and officers on half rations

The fourth order cut the extra rations issued at government expense to officers dramatically and reduced the number of women employed by each company from four to one. The soldiers employed the women as laundresses, cooks and other services.

The full rations per solder per day were:

1 pound of bread or flour

1 pound of beef or 3/4 pound of pork

1 gill of rum (4 fluid ounces)

1/100 quart of salt

1/50 quart of vinegar

1/50 pound of soap

1/100 pound of candle

St. Clair ordered Colonel Oldham use his regiment to escort the supply column headed to Fort Washington, however Oldham told St. Clair that his entire regiment would desert when they arrived at Fort Washington. St. Clair then charged Captain Faulkner and his Pennsylvania Riflemen with the task.

The cut in rations added to the general air of despair gathering over the army in the wilderness.

Newman's Journal

Captain Newman reported an incident in which three servants belonging to some of the officers had stolen horses and packed their belongings with the intention of fleeing to the Indians. Some militia riflemen captured them and brought them into camp.

October 20, 1791- Enlistments Begin to Run Out

Many of the troops that enlisted for the campaign had enlisted for six months. On October 20, the first of these levies ran out and about half of the soldiers in Virginia's First Levy Regiment, about 275 men, demanded that St. Clair discharge them. The General knew that if he tried to force them to stay, they would just refuse duty. They would consume valuable rations while contributing nothing. He also knew that other men in the regiment enlistments would expire during the next few days, so he decided to use the approximately 150 men to escort the pack horses back to Fort Washington and release them from duty there.

Captain Newman's Journal

Captain Newman records that he read some letters from home, written by his mother and other family and friends. He writes that he received a great deal of pleasure reading the letters and imagining them in various pursuits. He also reported that the weather was the coldest they had had so far.

October 21, 1791 - Twenty Men Desert

General St. Clair's army suffered the first mass desertion when twenty Kentucky militiamen deserted their posts. Their intent, it was clear, was to use the tracks of the returning herd of packhorses and their militia guards to cover their tracks.

Captain Newman's Journal

Captain Newman notes that the weather was very cold and there were snow flurries. He also reports that the General Court Martial board he had sat on had dissolved, having finished trying all the prisoners of capital crimes in possession.

October 22, 1791 - Deserters Captured

The twenty men that deserted from Fort Jefferson on October 21 had the bad luck to encounter a small packhorse convoy accompanied by an escort of sixty men. They captured the deserters and brought them back to the fort where they were held prisoner. The shipment of about 1800 pounds of flour was not nearly enough for the force of approximately 1400 men.

Captain Newman's Journal

Newman reports that the rations had been reduced further because of the scarcity of supplies. The order created more grumbling among the cold, hungry troops camped in the wilderness. The bulk of the work on Fort Jefferson was almost complete. Newman began preparing for the march, which would commence the next day. He would leave his extra baggage at the fort, as General St. Clair expected to move fast without baggage horses.

By the evening the soldiers had had completed the bulk of the work on Fort Jefferson.

October 23, 1791 - Three Soldiers Hung for Desertion

The weather had been clear and crisp for a couple of days. The soldiers arose and filed into the fort. They expected to attend a dedication ceremony. Instead, the grim spectacle of the hanging of three men who had committed capital crime became the first act in the new fort. The condemned included two officers who had deserted and a soldier that had threatened to shoot an officer. The execution completed, St. Clair chose the men that would serve to garrison the fort, who then filed in to take up quarters.

Captain Newman's Journal

Newman notes with relief that St. Clair had not chosen his company as a part of the garrison of the fort. He would leave much of his baggage behind, including his journal, as he prepared for the final push to Kekionga.

Author Note: October 23 is the last entry in Captain Samuel Newman's journal, providing a sad testament to his fate just over ten days later.

October 24, 1791 - St. Clair's Army Departs

Fort Jefferson measured about 115 feet square, with two blockhouses. However, the structure was not complete. Over the next year a corral, two more blockhouses, outbuildings and a garden would be built at the facility.

The Army Departs

Somewhere around 2000 troops had arrived at Fort Jefferson. Desertions, conscriptions running out and sickness had reduced the number of soldiers that left the fort to about 1400 soldiers, plus a 300-man group of Kentucky militia commanded by a Commander Oldham. Exact numbers of troops are sketchy and accounts vary from source to source. St. Clair had sent about 200 camp followers back to Fort Washington. About thirty women accompanied the force and an undetermined number of children. About ten or so civilian contractors accompanied the army. The camp diet and cold, damp weather had taken a toll on the fifty-four year old general. Afflicted by gout and in severe pain, he rode with the troops on a pallet that some soldiers had tied to a wagon bed. The first day the army marched about six miles along an Indian path that paralleled a creek that would later bear the name Greenville Creek. They marched through an open prairie and camped.

October 27, 1791 - Thirteen Men Demand Discharge

The army remained in camp waiting for supplies until October 28. The enlistments of the bulk of General St. Clair's army would expire on November 3. He had hoped to drive far enough into uncharted, dangerous country by that time that the men with expiring enlistments would be afraid to demand discharge and go home. Thirteen men from Virginia whose enlistments had expired demanded discharge on October 27. A supply wagon was due to arrive the next day and the general agreed to discharge them, but ordered them to stand escort for the packhorses when they returned to Fort Washington.

A Fading, Starving Army

The departing men would add to the list of men missing and presumed to have deserted or possibly abducted by Indians. The numbers of fighting men in St. Clair's army declined daily. Sporadic attacks on men while out hunting for food or forage for the horses added to the growing list of casualties. The horse's lack of hay or grass had taken its toll on the starving animals and on this date, the army had run completely out of flour. Bad as things were, things would get worse.

Scouts

This same day thirteen Chickasaw warriors arrived in camp to serve as scouts for the army. St. Clair welcomed them warmly, aware that until now he had a total lack of intelligence about the movements of his enemies. He hoped the warriors would fill that need. However, since the Chickasaw were from the Lower Mississippi area, they were unfamiliar with the terrain. It would take a few days for them to acclimate themselves well enough to enter service as scouts.

October 29, 1791 - St. Clair Deploys First Scouts

General St. Clair deployed the thirteen Chickasaw that had arrived with the army a few days before as scouts.

Chickasaw

The name Chickasaw derives from the word "Chikashsha" which translates as "rebel," or ""comes from Chicsa." Historians are uncertain of the ultimate origin of the Chickasaw nation. When Hernan De Soto encountered them on his 1540 expedition, the tribe occupied villages in the Lower Mississippi region in what is now Mississippi, Kentucky, Alabama and Tennessee. During colonial times, the Chickasaw lived an agricultural lifestyle and traded with the French and English colonists. The Chickasaw had allied with the English during the French and Indian War. Considered by the Americans as one of the Five Civilized Tribes, President George Washington considered the Indians equal with the American, but felt that their culture was inferior. Washington established programs during his administration designed to acclimate the native tribes with the European lifestyle in the hope that the natives and the Americans could live together in peace. The Five Civilized Tribes included the Chickasaw, Cherokee, Choctaw, Creek and Seminole. Washington took great pains to keep these tribes at peace with the United States during the Northwest Indian War. At the Treaty of Hopewell, the United States pledged to remain at peace with the Chickasaw. The Chickasaw and the Wabash tribes had been at war for about forty years.

October 31, 1791 - Sixty Men Desert

On October 31, sixty militiamen deserted the army, declaring that they would stop the next food convoy along the trail and confiscate the supplies. St. Clair, in desperation, sent 300 soldiers of the First United States Regiment to capture the deserters, protect the supply convoy and attempt to prevent further desertions. These men were St. Clair's most experienced and best fighters. They would not catch up with the deserters nor would they find the supply train at the point on the eighty-mile long wilderness trail St. Clair expected it. These 300 men would not arrive back time to participate in the battle on November 4.

Supply Convoy Arrives

Just before the sixty troops deserted, a convoy of 212 horses did arrive in camp. However, the weakened horses could only carry an average of 150 pounds of supplies each, about fifteen-ton total. The amount of supplies would only last the army about four days.

November 03, 1791 - St. Clair's Army Camped Along the Wabash River

By November 3, 1791, St. Clair reached the banks of a river he believed to be the St. Mary's River and about fifteen miles from Kekionga, and set up camp.

Bad Choices

Instead of the St Mary's, the army had reached the Wabash River and was about fifty-five miles from Kekionga. No maps of this wilderness region existed, and St. Clair operated with very little good intelligence. St. Clair chose to divide his forces, establishing the camps for the Kentucky militia and the regular Army troops and volunteers on opposite banks of he river. The camp stretched about 350 yards along both sides of the river. He ordered no fortifications built, nor did he deploy adequate sentries. The lack of fortifications left his artillery and his troops exposed. St. Clair still believed that, despite the desertions, he still maintained numerical superiority over his enemy. This, and the compact disposition of is force, he felt would discourage the Indians from attacking it. He went to bed believing that he was secure in his position and had the ability to choose when he would strike the Indians.

Warnings

During the night, unknown to St. Clair and his officers, over 1000 warriors, concealed by the dark and dense wilderness, crept in close to the unsuspecting army. The men on the outside fringes of the camp reported seeing them in the shadows. St. Clair's second in command, Major General Richard Butler, heard reports, and dispatched a force of about thirty men to scout. The scouts returned and reported that they believed that the warriors would attack in the morning. Apparently, Butler took no additional measures, nor did he wake General St. Clair. Historical lore indicates that he did not believe St. Clair was fit for duty because of his health and did not communicate with him well. The sentinels fired frequently during the night, spreading fear among the troops.

November 4, 1791 - St. Clair's Defeat or Battle of the Wabash

Sometime around 6:00 AM, the Indians struck hard and the battle did not last long.

The Battle of the Wabash

The warriors struck both camps separately and simultaneously, focusing their fire on the officers who were obvious by their different uniforms. The 270 men in the Kentucky militia fled as soon as the firing began. The

Indians cut the exposed artillerymen to pieces as they tried to man their weapons. What shots they did get off went over the heads of the natives, thus they were ineffective. Thus, Little Turtle's instructions to his disparate army of warriors had proved successful. The Indians had removed much of the army's leadership and eliminated the artillery threat. The veteran First Regiment had not returned from its expedition to capture the deserters, thus was not present for the battle. The Second Regiment had not been in battle before and took the brunt of the attack.

St. Clair During the Battle

The rush of adrenaline from the sounds of battle roused St. Clair from the pain of his illness. He rushed from his tent and acted with courage and firmness as he dealt with the fleeing militia and panicked women and children that had accompanied the army. After the battle, he found eight bullet holes in his cloak, though he remained untouched.

A Desperate Fight

They managed to hold out for a little over three hours. The number of battle ready troops shrank as the bodies of the dead and wounded littered the ground around them. The soldiers had not been ready for battle, and thus had only the standard issue of twenty-four cartridges with them. After about an hour or more, they began running out of ammunition and had to search through the dead and wounded men to find more ammunition.

Breakout

St. Clair realized his army was in jeopardy of total annihilation. He concentrated his force, which of course increased the casualty rate. The maneuver did enable him to charge the Indian's battle lines and push their way out. The desperate breakout forced the army to leave the dead and wounded behind. The success of the charge allowed St.

Clair, who had four horses shot out from under him, to lead the broken shards of his army south towards Fort Jefferson. The Indians pursued the fleeing army for about three miles before returning to the battlefield to loot the bodies. Captain Newman's company had been placed in charge of guarding the cattle and horses. Newman died sometime during the battle.

Hell on Earth

One young officer managed to escape death after the main army had fled by hiding in a hollow tree. From a knothole, he witnessed a horror on earth as the warriors stripped and scalped the dead. They left the wounded to suffer in pain and anguish until they had finished with the dead. Then they shot the wounded and plundered the bodies. The officer waited until darkness, then escaped into the wilderness to tell his tale.

First Regiment's Actions

Major John Hamtramck commanded the First Regiment. They had camped from between twenty and thirty miles to the south, probably near the future site of the future Fort Greenville. The distant sounds of battle reached the regiment. Hamtramck, knowing that St. Clair's army was engaged in battle, started immediately towards the sounds of battle. However, they soon encountered remnants of the fleeing militia, who relayed the news that an Indian force had surrounded the army and was destroying it. Hamtramck paused in his advance. If the Indians destroyed St. Clair's army, their next target would surely be the almost undefended Fort Jefferson. He made two decisions. He sent a small force towards the battle to get some solid news, and then proceeded with the bulk of his force back to fortify the post.

Survivors Return

The scout force encountered St. Clair and his fleeing army in mid afternoon. They accompanied them back to Fort Jefferson, arriving after nightfall. They completed the horrible march without food or water in the cold, and over frozen ground. St. Clair found the post overcrowded, with no food available. The next day he ordered the remaining men to return to Fort Hamilton, leaving the wounded, and those that had died of their wounds, behind. Over the next four days more survivors arrived at the fort, one having walked with a tomahawk embedded in is skull.

Worst United States Army Defeat in History

The magnitude of the defeat shocked the nation when reports filtered out. Thirty-nine out of fifty-two officers died in the battle, with another seven receiving wounds. Most of the 200 camp followers died in the carnage. 632 of the 920-army troops died with another 264 wounded. The casualty rate of over 97% remains the worst defeat, by percent, of the United States Army. It was, and would remain; the greatest military victory the Indians would have in their struggles to retain their land. A scant 24 soldiers escaped without harm. In a little over three hours the Indians had destroyed about one-fourth of the United States Army. During no single battle during the American Revolution had one battle cost so many lives.

Acknowledgements

January, 08 1782 - John Vawter Born (January 8, 1782 - August 17 1862)
Jennings Co, in - Pictorial
https://books.google.com/books?id=qHjs5nrluAAC&pg=PA20&lpg=PA20&dq=John+Va
wter+1816&source=bl&ots=_eZLsO6svF&sig=yjXk2-fzLmc7nZHGW-
nDingSawM&hl=en&sa=X&ved=0ahUKEwiOuqTTyabUAhVE4oMKHYtYCK0Q6AEILjAB
#v=onepage&q=John%20Vawter%201816&f=false
https://www.findagrave.com/memorial/52928295/john-vawter

February 01, 1783 - Site for Clark's Grant Indiana Selected
https://www.nps.gov/nr/travel/lewisandclark/ocs.htm
https://www.in.gov/history/2974.htm

April 08, 1783 - Jacob Whetzel Born - Whetzel Trace
http://www.in.gov/history/files/24.1965.1WhetzelsTrace.pdf
http://www.franklincountyhistoricalsociety.com/HM_Whetzel_Trace.html
http://www.shelbycountyindiana.org/biographies/bio_edward_toner.htm
http://www.findagrave.com/cgi-bin/fg.cgi?page=gr&GRid=20807098

July 02, 1783 - Virginia Relieves George Rogers Clark of his Command
https://en.wikipedia.org/wiki/George_Rogers_Clark
Four American Pioneers: Daniel Boone, George Rogers Clark, David Crockett ...
https://books.google.com/books?id=KYoWAAAAYAAJ&pg=PA128&lpg=PA128&dq=ge
orge+rogers+clark+relieved+of+command+1783&source=bl&ots=stNpTScT__&sig=YcAPP
U9jTg2bGXCy2QRIYVZmcPs&hl=en&sa=X&ved=0ahUKEwiZvZuEvc7TAhXo34MKHfZ4
CqIQ6AEITTAI#v=onepage&q=george%20rogers%20clark%20relieved%20of%20comman
d%201783&f=false
http://www.theodora.com/encyclopedia/c2/george_rogers_clark.html
http://www.biography.com/people/george-rogers-clark-9249343
https://en.wikipedia.org/wiki/Benjamin_Harrison_V

September 03, 1783 - Treaty of Paris signed - American War of Independence Over
http://www.ohiohistorycentral.org/w/Treaty_of_Paris_(1783)
https://www.ourdocuments.gov/doc.php?flash=true&doc=6
http://avalon.law.yale.edu/18th_century/paris.asp
March 1, 1784 - Virginia Cedes Claim to Virginia Territory to United States
https://en.wikipedia.org/wiki/Northwest_Ordinance
http://www.virginiaplaces.org/boundaries/cessions.html
http://www.in.gov/history/2898.htm
https://en.wikipedia.org/wiki/State_cessions

April 23, 1784 - Land Ordinance of 1784
http://www.u-s-history.com/pages/h1158.html
https://en.wikipedia.org/wiki/Land_Ordinance_of_1784

June 03, 1784 - First American Regiment Established
https://armyhistory.org/first-american-regiment/
http://www.oldfortsteuben.com/firstregiment.php
https://en.wikipedia.org/wiki/First_American_Regiment

October 22, 1784 - Treaty of Fort Stanwix (1784)
https://www.nps.gov/fost/learn/historyculture/treaty-landtransaction-1784.htm
https://en.wikipedia.org/wiki/Treaty_of_Fort_Stanwix_(1784)

http://pabook2.libraries.psu.edu/palitmap/Stanwix.html

December 06, 1785 - John Van Cleve Family Arrives Washington, Pennsylvania
https://www.findagrave.com/memorial/167585613/john-w.-van_cleve

January 21, 1785 - George Rogers Clark Helps Negotiate the Treaty of Fort McIntosh
https://beaverheritage.org/treaty-of-fort-mcintosh/
https://en.wikipedia.org/wiki/George_Rogers_Clark
http://www.ohiohistorycentral.org/w/Treaty_of_Fort_McIntosh_(1785)

May 20, 1785 - Land Ordinance of 1785
https://en.wikipedia.org/wiki/Land_Ordinance_of_1785
http://www.ohiohistorycentral.org/w/Land_Ordinance_of_1785?rec=1472

June 20, 1787 - Oliver Ellsworth Proposed the Name United States
http://www.let.rug.nl/usa/biographies/oliver-ellsworth/
https://en.wikipedia.org/wiki/Oliver_Ellsworth
https://www.thenewamerican.com/culture/history/item/21101-june-20-1787-defense-of-state-sovereignty-warning-against-con-cons
https://en.wikipedia.org/wiki/Oliver_Ellsworth
http://avalon.law.yale.edu/18th_century/debates_620.asp
https://blogs.loc.gov/law/2016/05/may-1787-the-beginning-of-the-constitutional-convention/
http://teachingamericanhistory.org/static/convention/delegates/ellsworth.html

August 25, 1795 - Northwest Territorial Assembly Adjourns - Maxwell's Code Becomes Law
https://books.google.com/books?id=5Rc9AAAAYAAJ&pg=PA392&lpg=PA392&dq=Maxwell%27s+Code+published&source=bl&ots=kyrqJr0Drc&sig=kmkWWrRs9Zk_CJVI2McUKzlSvRI&hl=en&sa=X&ved=0ahUKEwi0lcq3zvfLAhVI2SYKHUx-DPoQ6AEISzAI#v=onepage&q=Maxwell's%20Code%20published&f=false
https://doyle.com/auctions/14ba01-new-york-city-bar-association/catalogue/203-northwest-territory-maxwell-s-code-laws
http://www.genealogybug.net/ohio_alhn/OH_100yrs/laws_1795.shtml

October 22, 1785 - Fort Finney Established
http://www.whitewaterriverfoundation.org/PointsofInterest/fortfinney.html
https://www.jstor.org/stable/27570228?seq=1#page_scan_tab_contents
http://gehio.blogspot.com/2013/01/the-treaty-of-fort-finney.html
http://www.northbendohio.org/thevillageofnorthbendhistory.html
History of Dearborn and Ohio Counties, Indiana: From Their Earliest ..., Part 1
https://books.google.com/books?id=rCpEAQAAMAAJ&pg=PA78&lpg=PA78&dq=fort+finney+abandoned&source=bl&ots=P4jTpPi9d3&sig=nFDgrC7yw9eQ_xhyYVFwpDQY60w&hl=en&sa=X&ved=0ahUKEwjc6v_cq5HaAhUB9YMKHatvDfYQ6AEIdDAN#v=onepage&q=fort%20finney%20abandoned&f=false

August 15, - 1785   John Clark Purchases Farm Near Louisville, Kentucky
http://www.lewisandclarkinkentucky.org/places/mulberry_hill.shtml
http://filsonhistorical.org/then-and-now/
http://dgmweb.net/Resources/Bios/Bio-ClarkFamily-Jennings1929.html

January 31, 1786 - Treaty of Fort Finney
http://www.ohiohistorycentral.org/w/Treaty_of_Fort_Finney_(1786)
http://www.whitewaterriverfoundation.org/PointsofInterest/fortfinney.html

Indiana's Timeless Tales - 1782 – 1791

July 15, 1786 - Piankeshaw Warriors Return to Vincennes
The History of Indiana, from Its Earliest Exploration by Europeans, to the ...
https://books.google.com/books?id=yxEVAAAAYAAJ&pg=PA405&lpg=PA405&dq=Col
onel+LeGras&source=bl&ots=PataK7eNr3&sig=-WMAFC-
IiY7dODNlXaHfZOGAf0g&hl=en&sa=X&ved=0ahUKEwi9mP2L-
KLaAhUKi6wKHV1DCYAQ6AEIbjAM#v=onepage&q=Colonel%20LeGras&f=false
History of George Rogers Clark's conquest of the Illinois and the Wabash ...
https://books.google.com/books?id=bHoUAAAAYAAJ&pg=PA470&lpg=PA470&dq=Col
onel+LeGras&source=bl&ots=HxCNmyEM-
8&sig=Fdlio1vBDD1SczQ5g7uKBufx5Fw&hl=en&sa=X&ved=0ahUKEwi9mP2L-
KLaAhUKi6wKHV1DCYAQ6AEIcTAN#v=onepage&q=Colonel%20LeGras&f=false
https://en.wikipedia.org/wiki/Battle_of_the_Embarras_River
http://npshistory.com/series/symposia/george_rogers_clark/1991-1992/sec4.htm
http://npshistory.com/series/symposia/george_rogers_clark/1989-1990/sec3.htm
https://en.wikipedia.org/wiki/François_Riday_Busseron

July 15, 1786 - Piankeshaw Warriors Return to Vincennes
Jeffersonville, Indiana
http://en.wikipedia.org/wiki/Jeffersonville,_Indiana
http://www.cityofjeff.net/
http://www.historicjeffersonville.com/
http://www.jeffparks.org/
http://www.theriverstage.com/
http://www.fortwiki.com/Fort_Finney
http://indianaplaces.blogspot.com/2014/06/clark-county-indiana.html
https://ipfs.io/ipfs/QmXoypizjW3WknFiJnKLwHCnL72vedxjQkDDP1mXWo6uco/wiki/
Jeffersonville%2C_Indiana.html
https://en.wikipedia.org/wiki/Jeffersonville,_Indiana
Old Jeffersonville Historic Preservation Plan
http://www.in.gov/indot/files/090612_Final_Old_Jeff_HPP.pdf
https://en.wikipedia.org/wiki/Isaac_Bowman

November 06, 1786 - Isaac Blackford Born
http://www.in.gov/history/2547.htm
https://en.wikipedia.org/wiki/Isaac_Blackford

https://en.wikipedia.org/wiki/Timeline_of_drafting_and_ratification_of_the_United_Stat
es_Constitution
https://history.stackexchange.com/questions/15255/which-forts-did-the-british-keep-in-
the-northwest-territory-after-the-american-r
https://www.khanacademy.org/humanities/ap-us-history/period-3/apush-creating-a-
nation/a/the-constitutional-convention
https://www.loc.gov/rr/program/bib/ourdocs/Constitution.html

May 29, 1787 - Pinckney Plan Presented
https://en.wikipedia.org/wiki/Charles_Pinckney_(governor)
https://www.biography.com/people/charles-pinckney-9440930
https://en.wikipedia.org/wiki/Timeline_of_drafting_and_ratification_of_the_United_Stat
es_Constitution
https://beta.worldcat.org/archivegrid/record.php?id=146037691

May 25, 1787 - Constitutional Convention Meets - First Time
https://en.wikipedia.org/wiki/Timeline_of_drafting_and_ratification_of_the_United_Stat
es_Constitution

https://history.stackexchange.com/questions/15255/which-forts-did-the-british-keep-in-the-northwest-territory-after-the-american-r
https://www.khanacademy.org/humanities/ap-us-history/period-3/apush-creating-a-nation/a/the-constitutional-convention
https://www.loc.gov/rr/program/bib/ourdocs/Constitution.html

May 29, 1787 - Virginia Plan Presented
http://www.let.rug.nl/usa/biographies/edmund-randolph/
https://en.wikipedia.org/wiki/Edmund_Randolph
https://en.wikipedia.org/wiki/Timeline_of_drafting_and_ratification_of_the_United_States_Constitution
https://founders.archives.gov/documents/Madison/01-10-02-0005
https://www.ourdocuments.gov/doc.php?flash=true&doc=7
https://en.wikipedia.org/wiki/Virginia_Plan

June 15, 1787 - New Jersey Plan Presented
http://bioguide.congress.gov/scripts/biodisplay.pl?index=p000102
https://www.geni.com/people/Gov-William-Paterson/6000000000985588776
https://en.wikipedia.org/wiki/Timeline_of_drafting_and_ratification_of_the_United_States_Constitution

July 16, 1787 - Connecticut Compromise Approved by Committee
https://en.wikipedia.org/wiki/Timeline_of_drafting_and_ratification_of_the_United_States_Constitution
http://teachingamericanhistory.org/convention/summary/

June 18, 1787 - Hamilton Plan Presented
https://en.wikipedia.org/wiki/Timeline_of_drafting_and_ratification_of_the_United_States_Constitution
https://www.usconstitution.net/plan_brit.html
https://www.heritage.org/political-process/report/alexander-hamilton-and-american-progressivism

July 7, 1787 - Harmar Departs Falls of the Ohio for Vincennes
Warrick County Prior to 1818
Arvil S. Barr
https://www.jstor.org/stable/27785873?seq=1#page_scan_tab_contents
https://scholarworks.iu.edu/journals/index.php/imh/article/view/9164/12041
http://npshistory.com/series/symposia/george_rogers_clark/1989-1990/sec3.htm
August 06, 1787 - Constitutional Convention Reconvenes
http://teachingamericanhistory.org/convention/summary/

July 24, 1787 - Committee of Five Appointed to Write First Draft   of Constitution
https://www.loc.gov/collections/continental-congress-and-constitutional-convention-from-1774-to-1789/articles-and-essays/to-form-a-more-perfect-union/creating-a-constitution/
https://en.wikipedia.org/wiki/Constitutional_Convention_(United_States)
http://teachingamericanhistory.org/convention/summary/

September 15, 1787 - Constitutional Convention Approves the United States Constitution
http://teachingamericanhistory.org/convention/summary/

Indiana's Timeless Tales - 1782 – 1791

September 17, 1787 - Constitutional Convention Adjourns
http://teachingamericanhistory.org/convention/summary/
http://teachingamericanhistory.org/library/document/benjamin-franklins-speech-federal-convention/

October 03, 1787 - Major John Hamtrampk Appointed Commander of Vincennes
https://books.google.com/books?id=zBQVAAAAYAAJ&pg=PA239&lpg=PA239&dq=har
mar+arrives+vincennes+1787&source=bl&ots=T3Wv63qN2d&sig=31GK5ZfnBigmKxbFpr
ZVkJ81SVQ&hl=en&sa=X&ved=0ahUKEwjnyIaCzL7aAhVP_oMKHbnZAY44ChDoAQgx
MAI#v=onepage&q=harmar%20arrives%20vincennes%201787&f=false
https://www.findagrave.com/memorial/14862717/jean-francois-hamtramck
https://www.geni.com/people/Col-Jean-François-Hamtramck/6000000030753614892
https://en.wikipedia.org/wiki/Jean_François_Hamtramck
https://www.in.gov/history/markers/167.htm
https://scholarworks.iu.edu/journals/index.php/imh/article/view/9164/12042

October 05, 1787, General Arthur St. Clair Chosen Governor of Northwest Territory
Ohio Interrogations Points
https://books.google.com/books?id=jfOgAAAAMAAJ&pg=PA7&lpg=PA7&dq=First+Le
gislative+Assembly+of+Northwest+Territory+1799&source=bl&ots=Fu_29Xf9p4&sig=ul8
mjD7EPDFKo1zqMtT8UVhnGho&hl=en&sa=X&ved=0ahUKEwjQlKWKy4jVAhVI5SYKH
UN9BCIQ6AEIQjAD#v=onepage&q=First%20Legislative%20Assembly%20of%20Northwe
st%20Territory%201799&f=false
https://en.wikipedia.org/wiki/Northwest_Territory
https://en.wikipedia.org/wiki/Arthur_St._Clair
http://www.ohiohistorycentral.org/w/Arthur_St._Clair
http://www.mountvernon.org/digital-encyclopedia/article/arthur-st-clair/
Territory to Statehood PDF

April 07, 1788 - Marietta, Ohio Established - First Seat of Northwest Territory Government
Ohio Interrogation Points
https://books.google.com/books?id=jfOgAAAAMAAJ&pg=PA7&lpg=PA7&dq=First+Le
gislative+Assembly+of+Northwest+Territory+1799&source=bl&ots=Fu_29Xf9p4&sig=ul8
mjD7EPDFKo1zqMtT8UVhnGho&hl=en&sa=X&ved=0ahUKEwjQlKWKy4jVAhVI5SYKH
UN9BCIQ6AEIQjAD#v=onepage&q=First%20Legislative%20Assembly%20of%20Northwe
st%20Territory%201799&f=false
https://en.wikipedia.org/wiki/Marietta,_Ohio

July 09, 1788 - General St. Clair Arrives Marietta
https://books.google.com/books?id=jfOgAAAAMAAJ&pg=PA7&lpg=PA7&dq=First+Le
gislative+Assembly+of+Northwest+Territory+1799&source=bl&ots=Fu_29Xf9p4&sig=ul8
mjD7EPDFKo1zqMtT8UVhnGho&hl=en&sa=X&ved=0ahUKEwjQlKWKy4jVAhVI5SYKH
UN9BCIQ6AEIQjAD#v=onepage&q=First%20Legislative%20Assembly%20of%20Northwe
st%20Territory%201799&f=false
https://en.wikipedia.org/wiki/Marietta,_Ohio
https://en.wikipedia.org/wiki/Northwest_Territory

April 10, 1788 - William Paul Quinn Born
https://www.fs.usda.gov/recarea/hoosier/recarea/?recid=81889

July 26, 1788 First Use of the Official Northwest Territory Seal
http://www.in.gov/history/2804.htm

December 15, 1798 - First Election Northwest Territory
http://moodle.doe.in.gov/calendar/view.php?view=month&course=1&time=-5714388000
Ohio Interrogation Points
https://books.google.com/books?id=jfOgAAAAMAAJ&pg=PA7&lpg=PA7&dq=First+Le
gislative+Assembly+of+Northwest+Territory+1799&source=bl&ots=Fu_29Xf9p4&sig=ul8
mjD7EPDFKo1zqMtT8UVhnGho&hl=en&sa=X&ved=0ahUKEwjQlKWKy4jVAhVI5SYKH
UN9BCIQ6AEIQjAD#v=onepage&q=First%20Legislative%20Assembly%20of%20Northwe
st%20Territory%201799&f=false

December 28, 1788 - Losantiville (Cincinnati) Established
http://library.cincymuseum.org/cincifaq.htm

1788 - Francis Godfrey Born
https://en.wikipedia.org/wiki/Francis_Godfroy

Vincennes Donation Lands
http://scholarworks.iu.edu/journals/index.php/imh/article/view/7861/9435

February 04, 1789 - George Washington Elected President
https://www.archives.gov/federal-register/electoral-college/scores.html
https://www.history.com/this-day-in-history/george-washington-is-elected-president
https://www.mountvernon.org/george-washington/the-first-president/election/10-facts-
about-washingtons-election/
https://en.wikipedia.org/wiki/United_States_presidential_election,_1788–89

February 06, 1789 - First Marriage in Newly Organized Northwest Territory
Yankee Colonies across America: Cities upon the Hills
https://books.google.com/books?id=LSBUCwAAQBAJ&pg=PA29&lpg=PA29&dq=first+
marriage+northwest+territory+1789&source=bl&ots=RfbToLaCHd&sig=xSMgikrzeZ0guP
7TObd7WgTHRg0&hl=en&sa=X&ved=0ahUKEwjl59GEytLaAhVI6YMKHePOCOoQ6AEI
ejAK#v=onepage&q=first%20marriage%20northwest%20territory%201789&f=false
https://en.wikipedia.org/wiki/Northwest_Territory
https://www.findagrave.com/memorial/94843598/rowena-sargeant

July 27, 1789 - John Cleve Moves to Crawford's Ford
https://www.findagrave.com/memorial/167585613/john-w.-van_cleve

August 09, 1789 - Army Troops Arrive at North Bend to Construct Fort Washington
https://www.geni.com/people/General-D-E-A-Strong/6000000000584429920
http://www.ohiohistorycentral.org/w/Cincinnati,_Ohio
http://npshistory.com/series/symposia/george_rogers_clark/1989-1990/sec4.htm
https://www.findagrave.com/memorial/89379154/david-strong
https://en.wikipedia.org/wiki/John_Doughty

http://genealogytrails.com/ohio/hamilton/history_thestoryofhamilton.html

January 02, 1790 - Hamilton County Established - Ohio
http://www.ohiohistorycentral.org/index.php?title=Hamilton_County&mobileaction=tog
gle_view_mobile
https://hcgsohio.org/cpage.php?pt=39
https://en.wikipedia.org/wiki/Alexander_Hamilton

Indiana's Timeless Tales - 1782 – 1791

January 04, 1790 - St. Clair Renames Lonsantiville to Cincinnati
https://en.wikipedia.org/wiki/Lucius_Quinctius_Cincinnatus
http://www.ohiohistorycentral.org/w/Cincinnati,_Ohio
http://npshistory.com/series/symposia/george_rogers_clark/1989-1990/sec4.htm
https://en.wikipedia.org/wiki/Lucius_Quinctius_Cincinnatus

March 16, 1790 - Hamtramck Dispatches Peace Message up the Wabash
The Miami Indians
By Bert Anson
https://books.google.com/books?id=zOKgGQeETn4C&pg=PA110&lpg=PA110&dq=Ham
tramck+vincennes+1790&source=bl&ots=MBZ8PTiUrn&sig=xVfbsNe8m2Xn2kg6qayEoVS
gEos&hl=en&sa=X&ved=0ahUKEwjwyvSMq-
TaAhVYyYMKHXTpBt0Q6AEIYDAI#v=onepage&q=Hamtramck%20vincennes%201790&f
=false

April 05, 1790 - Antoine Gamelin Sent to Ouiatenon
http://purl.dlib.indiana.edu/iudl/imh/resource/xml/imh_issue.dtd
Readings in Indiana history
https://books.google.com/books?id=LhcVAAAAYAAJ&pg=PA68&lpg=PA68&dq=Antoi
ne+Gamelin+vincennes&source=bl&ots=-
of67tbBup&sig=DovVEyIVROOvXPeJCS6FJki8CVc&hl=en&sa=X&ved=0ahUKEwiI28yVv
9XbAhUC0FMKHS_fAhwQ6AEINDAD#v=onepage&q=Antoine%20Gamelin%20vincenne
s&f=false
https://www.wikitree.com/wiki/Gamelin-185

April 09, 1790 - Gamelin Reaches the Village of the Piankeshaw
http://www.ohiohistorycentral.org/w/Piankashaw_Indians
http://wardepartmentpapers.org/document.php?id=4390
https://en.wikipedia.org/wiki/Piankeshaw

April 11, 1790 - Gamelin Visits Kickapoo Village
http://wardepartmentpapers.org/document.php?id=4390

April 18, 1790 - Harmar Begins Scioto Campaign
https://books.google.com/books?id=bkJSi9g8ZQQC&pg=PA366&lpg=PA366&dq=attack
+scioto+may+1790+harmar&source=bl&ots=0HghpKZV5Y&sig=E2iiOrkPTCTlUCc3Y7wY
zbam_eI&hl=en&sa=X&ved=2ahUKEwjM3NHJ18bdAhUhxYMKHepGBeQQ6AEwBnoEC
AAQAQ#v=onepage&q=attack%20scioto%20may%201790%20harmar&f=false
http://wardepartmentpapers.org/document.php?id=4462
http://wardepartmentpapers.org/document.php?id=4201

July 15, 1790 - General Harmar Outlines His Battle Plan Against Kekionga
http://www.genealogycenter.org/Community/Blog/acpl-genealogy-
blog/2013/06/18/The_Origins_of_"Kekionga"_in_Fort_Wayne_s_Past_Pt_1
https://archfw.org/heritagetrail/kekionga/kekionga/
http://www.dtic.mil/get-tr-doc/pdf?AD=AD1001665
"Our Loss Was Heavy": Brigadier General Josiah Harmar's Kekionga Campaign of 1790
A Monograph
by
MAJ (P) Edwin D. Matthaidess III
United States Army

July 23, 1790 - The Intercourse Act
https://www.encyclopedia.com/history/encyclopedias-almanacs-transcripts-and-maps/us-congress-act-regulate-trade-and-intercourse-indian-tribes
http://pages.uoregon.edu/mjdennis/courses/hist469_trade.htm

September 22, 1790 - Hamtramck Departs Vincennes
https://en.wikipedia.org/wiki/Jean_François_Hamtramck
The Miami Indians
By Bert Anson
https://books.google.com/books?id=zOKgGQeETn4C&pg=PA110&lpg=PA110&dq=Hamtramck+vincennes+1790&source=bl&ots=MBZ8PTiUrn&sig=xVfbsNe8m2Xn2kg6qayEoVSgEos&hl=en&sa=X&ved=0ahUKEwjwyvSMq-TaAhVYyYMKHXTpBt0Q6AEIYDAI#v=onepage&q=Hamtramck%20vincennes%201790&f=false
https://en.wikipedia.org/wiki/Jean_François_Hamtramck

September 28, 1790 - The State of the Army
http://warfarehistorynetwork.com/daily/military-history/northwest-indian-war-marching-against-little-turtle/
http://www.ohiohistorycentral.org/w/Harmar%27s_Defeat

September 26, 1790 - Harmar's Force Leaves Fort Washington
https://en.wikipedia.org/wiki/Harmar_Campaign
http://www.dtic.mil/get-tr-doc/pdf?AD=AD1001665
"Our Loss Was Heavy": Brigadier General Josiah Harmar's Kekionga Campaign of 1790
A Monograph
by
MAJ (P) Edwin D. Matthaidess III

October 22, 1790 - Battle of Pumpkin Fields
https://www.boonesociety.com/pages/saving-private-boone/
http://warfarehistorynetwork.com/daily/military-history/northwest-indian-war-marching-against-little-turtle/
http://gehio.blogspot.com/2014/10/battle-of-pumpkin-fields.html

January 02, 1791 - Attack at Big Bottom - Muskingum River
http://www.ohiohistorycentral.org/w/Big_Bottom_Massacre
Charles Scott's March on Ouiatenon Document
https://founders.archives.gov/documents/Washington/05-07-02-0115

January 08, 1791 - Surveyors Attacked near Dunlap's Station
http://www.ancientohiotrail.org/support/pdfs/Great_Miami.pdf
https://ss.sites.mtu.edu/mhugl/2015/10/11/dunlaps-station/
http://www.colerainehistorical-oh.org/township-history/
http://www.mvreenactors.com/dunlap.html

January 23, 1791 - Governor Arthur St. Clair Sends Message to Major John Hamtramck
http://wardepartmentpapers.org/document.php?id=4390
Readings in Indiana history
https://books.google.com/books?id=LhcVAAAAYAAJ&pg=PA68&lpg=PA68&dq=Antoine+Gamelin+vincennes&source=bl&ots=-of67tbBup&sig=DovVEyIVROOvXPeJCS6FJki8CVc&hl=en&sa=X&ved=0ahUKEwiI28yVv9XbAhUC0FMKHS_fAhwQ6AEINDAD#v=onepage&q=Antoine%20Gamelin%20vincennes&f=false

Indiana's Timeless Tales - 1782 – 1791

March 09, 1790 - Isreal Ludlow Establishes Ludlow's Station
https://www.hmdb.org/marker.asp?marker=78961
https://books.google.com/books?id=eJxABLtxX60C&pg=PA281&lpg=PA281&dq=ludlow
+station+1790&source=bl&ots=e8a82PiTF5&sig=CN-xI-
IOxivPPqdOMTcABz0VPEg&hl=en&sa=X&ved=2ahUKEwjo2py-
ndjcAhWsz4MKHSsqB3cQ6AEwBnoECAQQAQ#v=onepage&q=ludlow%20station%2017
90&f=false
http://www.ohiohistorycentral.org/index.php?title=Hamilton_County&mobileaction=tog
gle_view_mobile
https://www.geni.com/people/Col-Israel-Ludlow/6000000043716851476
http://www.ohiohistorycentral.org/w/Israel_Ludlow

April 05, 1791 - Antoine Gamelin Sent to Ouiatenon
http://purl.dlib.indiana.edu/iudl/imh/resource/xml/imh_issue.dtd
Readings in Indiana history
https://books.google.com/books?id=LhcVAAAAYAAJ&pg=PA68&lpg=PA68&dq=Antoi
ne+Gamelin+vincennes&source=bl&ots=-
of67tbBup&sig=DovVEyIVROOvXPeJCS6FJki8CVc&hl=en&sa=X&ved=0ahUKEwiI28yVv
9XbAhUC0FMKHS_fAhwQ6AEINDAD#v=onepage&q=Antoine%20Gamelin%20vincenne
s&f=false
https://www.wikitree.com/wiki/Gamelin-185

April 07, 1790 - General Josiah Harmar Report on Shawnee Attacks on the Ohio River
William Wells and the Struggle for the Old Northwest
https://books.google.com/books?id=dwAxBwAAQBAJ&pg=PA87&lpg=PA87&dq=attack
+march+1790+scioto+river&source=bl&ots=wMPM-
Z3IbW&sig=9QAwFqttuaRrXdeIKUT6Q-
KGx4o&hl=en&sa=X&ved=2ahUKEwik4smA0MbdAhXo6IMKHf7vBpYQ6AEwBHoECAY
QAQ#v=onepage&q=attack%20march%201790%20scioto%20river&f=false
http://wardepartmentpapers.org/searchresults.php?searchClass=fulltextSearch&fulltextQ
uery=Big+Limestone+River
http://wardepartmentpapers.org/document.php?id=4248
http://wardepartmentpapers.org/document.php?id=4247
http://wardepartmentpapers.org/document.php?id=4201

April 09, 1790 - Gamelin Reaches the Village of the Piankeshaw
http://www.ohiohistorycentral.org/w/Piankashaw_Indians
http://wardepartmentpapers.org/document.php?id=4390
https://en.wikipedia.org/wiki/Piankeshaw

December 30, 1790 - Virginia Governor Establishes Kentucky Board of War
Historical Memory and Representations of the Vietnam War
edited by Walter L. Hixson
https://books.google.com/books?id=W_StoqYjC-sC&pg=RA1-PA369&lpg=RA1-
PA369&dq=kentucky+board+of+war+december+30+1790&source=bl&ots=DAY-
A6uXi_&sig=pMBzmDM_7UnDO4bl-
YirxLFTWZU&hl=en&sa=X&ved=2ahUKEwjsp8qYsPHcAhVI5YMKHYevCKsQ6AEwAno
ECAgQAQ#v=onepage&q=kentucky%20board%20of%20war%20december%2030%201790
&f=false
http://athena.uky.edu/kyleidoscope/newstateky/county/county.htm

March 03, 1791 - Congress Approves Enlargement of the Army
https://history.army.mil/books/RevWar/ss/repdoc.htm
https://en.wikisource.org/wiki/United_States_Statutes_at_Large/Volume_1/1st_Congress/3rd_Session/Chapter_28
http://warfarehistorynetwork.com/daily/military-history/northwest-indian-war-marching-against-little-turtle/

March 04, 1791 - Samuel Hodgdon Appointed as Quartermaster General
https://www.myheritage.com/names/samuel_hodgdon
http://old.qmfound.com/Samuel_Hodgdon.htm
http://npshistory.com/series/symposia/george_rogers_clark/1983-1984/sec6.htm
http://www.quartermaster.army.mil/bios/previous-qm-generals/quartermaster_general_bio-hodgdon.html

March 10, 1791 - Thomas Proctor Receives Commission for Peace Mission
http://www.waymarking.com/waymarks/WMC7G_FORT_FRANKLIN
https://en.wikipedia.org/wiki/Thomas_Proctor_(general)
http://www.ushistory.org/carpentershall/history/proctermission.htm
http://wardepartmentpapers.org/searchresults.php?searchClass=fulltextSearch&fulltextQuery=Thomas+Proctor
http://www.houseofproctor.org/genealogy/showmedia.php?mediaID=8568&medialinkID=7973
https://www.geni.com/people/Colonel-Thomas-Proctor/6000000010697628851
http://wardepartmentpapers.org/searchresults.php?searchClass=fulltextSearch&fulltextQuery=Colonel%20Thomas%20Proctor&orderBy=&page=2
http://wardepartmentpapers.org/searchresults.php?searchClass=fulltextSearch&fulltextQuery=John+Jeffers+1791&submitSearchSimple=Search&orderBy=&page=1
A History of Wilkes-Barré, Luzerne County, Pennsylvania: From Its ..., Volume 5
https://books.google.com/books?id=xLBZAAAAYAAJ&pg=PA1130&lpg=PA1130&dq=Buffalo+Creek,+procter+1791&source=bl&ots=kdhye7yTtB&sig=XqWwSTWfhPImvF3rm8w7Lb2FFH0&hl=en&sa=X&ved=0ahUKEwiVp_2185HcAhUo9IMKHVMLDq0Q6AEISDAF#v=onepage&q=Buffalo%20Creek%2C%20procter%201791&f=false

March 19, 1791 - Thomas Proctor Arrives at Wilkesburg
Thomas Proctor Journal
http://files.usgwarchives.net/pa/1pa/history/local/proctor01.txt
https://en.wikipedia.org/wiki/Tinderbox
https://en.wikipedia.org/wiki/Pyrite
https://en.wikipedia.org/wiki/Flint
https://en.wikipedia.org/wiki/Char_cloth
https://en.wikipedia.org/wiki/Match

March 20, 1791 - Thomas Proctor Arrives at Captain Waterman Baldwin's Home
http://www.americanrevolution.org/4thct.php
https://www.findagrave.com/memorial/45396008/waterman-baldwin
http://valleyforgemusterroll.org/regiments/ct4.asp
https://www.geni.com/people/Waterman-Baldwin/6000000001544403408
Index of the Rolls of Honor (ancestor's Index) in the Lineage ..., Volumes 55-56
https://books.google.com/books?id=7NJKAAAAYAAJ&pg=PA219&lpg=PA219&dq=Waterman+Baldwin+1757&source=bl&ots=Rq5zlDPEwp&sig=XNOhi160fODssluoQuD-YlSglVw&hl=en&sa=X&ved=0ahUKEwjxj9SZ8JvcAhUGxoMKHfLFDx0Q6AEINTAD#v=onepage&q=Waterman%20Baldwin%201757&f=false

Indiana's Timeless Tales - 1782 – 1791

March 22, 1791 - Proctor's Party Arrives at Buttermilk Falls
https://en.wikipedia.org/wiki/Buttermilk_Creek_(Susquehanna_River)
http://www.pawaterfalls.com/buttermilk_wyoming.html

March 26, 1791 - Proctor's Party Arrives at Tioga Point
Thomas Proctor Journal
http://files.usgwarchives.net/pa/1pa/history/local/proctor01.txt

April 06, 1791 - Cornplanter Visits Proctor Fort Franklin
https://en.wikipedia.org/wiki/Cornplanter
http://explorepahistory.com/hmarker.php?markerId=1-A-22D
Thomas Proctor Journal
http://files.usgwarchives.net/pa/1pa/history/local/proctor01.txt

April 13, 1791 - Proctor's Party Departs Fort Franklin for Buffalo Creek
Thomas Proctor Journal
http://files.usgwarchives.net/pa/1pa/history/local/proctor01.txt
April 27, 1791 - Proctor's Party Arrives at Buffalo Creek
Documents of the Assembly of the State of New York
https://books.google.com/books?id=dXhj8LLRH5kC&pg=RA1-PA374&lpg=RA1-
PA374&dq=Dunewangua&source=bl&ots=fl4-nxeEEJ&sig=FB74sISFUqIXEV-
okZP4El1unGA&hl=en&sa=X&ved=0ahUKEwjfmYLnqajcAhUk64MKHekMAeMQ6AEIO
DAF#v=onepage&q=Dunewangua&f=false
https://www.findagrave.com/memorial/150468216/ahweyneyonh
https://en.wikipedia.org/wiki/Red_Jacket
https://www.findagrave.com/memorial/3602/red_jacket
Thomas Proctor Journal
http://files.usgwarchives.net/pa/1pa/history/local/proctor01.txt

May 05, 1791 - Thomas Rhea Captured at Cassawago
American State Papers: Documents, Legislative and ..., Part 2, Volume 1
By United States. Congress
https://books.google.com/books?id=rogbAQAAMAAJ&pg=PA196&lpg=PA196&dq=tho
mas+rhea+sandusky+1791&source=bl&ots=UM64RJLqzt&sig=Ep09WSYNOa_H6TsSYgfG
GFkVuy8&hl=en&sa=X&ved=2ahUKEwiT_r_dk87cAhXj6IMKHT2eDaMQ6AEwAnoECA
gQAQ#v=onepage&q=thomas%20rhea%20sandusky%201791&f=false
https://en.wikipedia.org/wiki/Meadville,_Pennsylvania
http://genealogytrails.com/penn/venango/history/index.html
https://en.wikipedia.org/wiki/Meadville,_Pennsylvania
Historical Collections, Volume 24
https://books.google.com/books?id=P5cUAAAAYAAJ&pg=PA277&lpg=PA277&dq=Tho
mas+Rhea+sandusky+1791&source=bl&ots=A6vkb72XzG&sig=Ox1pokNch_vJ3u0UyYL4
Gb_ebRA&hl=en&sa=X&ved=2ahUKEwiHr8WAj87cAhVS1IMKHY5UBBQQ6AEwBXoEC
AUQAQ#v=onepage&q=Thomas%20Rhea%20sandusky%201791&f=false

May 15, 1791 - St. Clair Arrives Fort Washington
The Soldiers of America's First Army, 1791
https://books.google.com/books?id=UDxBU0JfgjMC&pg=PA62&lpg=PA62&dq=fort+ha
milton+september+19+1791&source=bl&ots=4plbLozxT4&sig=rjZuCbWNbxhBXE_0IYj_b0
G9Si0&hl=en&sa=X&ved=2ahUKEwjViaX11cbcAhXl3YMKHVZ4DnUQ6AEwBHoECAQQ
AQ#v=onepage&q=fort%20hamilton%20september%2019%201791&f=false
http://npshistory.com/series/symposia/george_rogers_clark/1983-1984/sec6.htm

May 18, 1775 - Benedict Arnold Captures Fort St. Johns
http://www.revolutionaryday.com/usroute4/whitehall/default.htm
https://en.wikibooks.org/wiki/American_Revolution/Ticonderoga_and_Bunker_Hill
https://www.americanheritage.com/content/why-benedict-arnold-did-it

May 21, 1791 - John Van Cleve Shot at in his Fields
http://wardepartmentpapers.org/document.php?id=4247
https://www.findagrave.com/memorial/167585613/john-w.-van_cleve
http://wardepartmentpapers.org/searchresults.php?searchClass=fulltextSearch&fulltextQ
uery=Big+Limestone+River

May 22, 1791 - Major-General Richard Butler Arrives at Fort Pitt
https://www.werelate.org/wiki/Person:Captain_Butler_%281%29
https://en.wikipedia.org/wiki/Richard_Butler_(general)
https://sites.google.com/a/lanepl.org/columns-by-jim-blount/2016-articles/-provision-
of-tools-scanty-in-the-extreme-for-soldiers-assigned-to-build-fort-hamilton

May 23, 1791 - General Scott Begins March to Fort Ouiatenon
Indiana Magazine of History
General Charles Scott and His March To Ouiatenon
http://purl.dlib.indiana.edu/iudl/imh/resource/xml/imh_issue.dtd
https://en.wikipedia.org/wiki/Muskingum_River
https://en.wikipedia.org/wiki/Fort_Harmar

June 1, 1791 - Destruction of Fort Ouiatenon
Indiana Magazine of History
General Charles Scott and His March To Ouiatenon
http://purl.dlib.indiana.edu/iudl/imh/resource/xml/imh_issue.dtd
https://www.in.gov/idem/nps/files/wmp_bigpine_sects_1-2.pdf
https://en.wikipedia.org/wiki/Fort_Ouiatenon
https://www.tippecanoehistory.org/our-places/blockhouse-museum/
https://scholarworks.iu.edu/journals/index.php/imh/article/view/6361/6438
https://www.in.gov/idem/nps/files/wmp_bigpine_sects_1-2.pdf

https://en.wikipedia.org/wiki/Ouiatenon
http://www.tolatsga.org/kick.html
June 04, 1791 - Scott Released Prisoners
Indiana Magazine of History
General Charles Scott and His March To Ouiatenon
http://purl.dlib.indiana.edu/iudl/imh/resource/xml/imh_issue.dtd

June 25, 1791 - St. Clair Requests Kentucky Send Another Expedition Against Natives
The Voice of the Frontier: John Bradford's Notes on Kentucky
edited by Thomas D. Clark
https://books.google.com/books?id=hr8eBgAAQBAJ&pg=PA150&lpg=PA150&dq=st.+Cl
air+letter+june+25+1791&source=bl&ots=YhfbICeThm&sig=42ZPoRLUMlTy-
N2zIB0YtAn3xTQ&hl=en&sa=X&ved=2ahUKEwiahfPQ5tDcAhUK24MKHVkPCVYQ6AE
wBHoECAYQAQ#v=onepage&q=st.%20Clair%20letter%20june%2025%201791&f=false
Warfare in the USA 1784861
edited by Samuel Watson
https://books.google.com/books?id=vexHDwAAQBAJ&pg=PT160&lpg=PT160&dq=Keth
tipecanunck&source=bl&ots=m_IOL-1nJD&sig=e50fO6coDbL5y1-ec5WgErrc-
tw&hl=en&sa=X&ved=2ahUKEwigvPGz7encAhUC7YMKHcnyDj8Q6AEwAXoECAkQAQ
#v=onepage&q=Kethtipecanunck&f=false

Land of the Miamis
Elmore Barce
https://books.google.com/books?id=8rHUiMGfIqQC&printsec=titlepage#v=onepage&q&f=false

July 01, 1791 - Blacksmith John Van Cleve Killed and Scalped Outside Fort Washington
https://www.findagrave.com/memorial/167585613/john-w.-van_cleve

A Picture of the First United States Army: The Journal of Captain Samuel Newman
https://www.jstor.org/stable/4630126?seq=3#page_scan_tab_contents
Journal Article

July 10, 1791 - Scheduled Departure of St. Clair's Army

August 04, 1791 - Newman's Company Camps at Lancaster
Captain Newman's Journal
http://content.wisconsinhistory.org/cdm/ref/collection/wmh/id/829

August 07, 1791 - Battle of Kenapacomaqua
https://en.wikipedia.org/wiki/Battle_of_Kenapacomaqua
http://incass-inmiami.org/cass/cemeteries/abnd/olde_towne/
http://casscountyin.tripod.com/CCHS/CC_History.html
https://en.wikisource.org/wiki/Lieut._Colonel-commandant_Wilkinson%27s_Report,_August_24,_1791
http://history.hanover.edu/hhr/98/hhr98_1.html

August 09, 1791 - Wilkinson Destroys Kethtipecanunck
Land of the Miamis
Elmore Barce
https://books.google.com/books?id=8rHUiMGfIqQC&printsec=titlepage#v=onepage&q&f=false
August 11, 1791 - Newman's Company Stops Due to Heavy Rain
Captain Newman's Journal
http://content.wisconsinhistory.org/cdm/ref/collection/wmh/id/829

August 14, 1791 - Captain Newman Reclaims Two Prisoners at Chambersburg
Captain Newman's Journal
http://content.wisconsinhistory.org/cdm/ref/collection/wmh/id/829

August 17, 1791- Provision Wagon Breaks Down - Captain Newman's Journal
Captain Newman's Journal
http://content.wisconsinhistory.org/cdm/ref/collection/wmh/id/829

August 19, 1791 - The March Continues - Captain Newman's Journal
Captain Newman's Journal
http://content.wisconsinhistory.org/cdm/ref/collection/wmh/id/829

August 25, 1795 - Northwest Territorial Assembly Adjourns - Maxwell's Code Becomes Law
https://books.google.com/books?id=5Rc9AAAAYAAJ&pg=PA392&lpg=PA392&dq=Max
well%27s+Code+published&source=bl&ots=kyrqJr0Drc&sig=kmkWWrRs9Zk_CJVI2McU
KzlSvRI&hl=en&sa=X&ved=0ahUKEwi0lcq3zvfLAhVI2SYKHUx-
DPoQ6AEISzAI#v=onepage&q=Maxwell's%20Code%20published&f=false
https://doyle.com/auctions/14ba01-new-york-city-bar-association/catalogue/203-
northwest-territory-maxwell-s-code-laws
http://www.genealogybug.net/ohio_alhn/OH_100yrs/laws_1795.shtml

August 27, 1791 - Newman's Company Arrives Fort Pitt - Captain Newman's Journal
Captain Newman's Journal
http://content.wisconsinhistory.org/cdm/ref/collection/wmh/id/829

September 05, 1791 - Captain Samuel Newman Departs Fort Pitt
https://www.jstor.org/stable/4630126?seq=3#page_scan_tab_contents
https://www.jstor.org/stable/pdf/4630127.pdf?refreqid=excelsior%3A73e57da832a28e93
5dd14d4410971198
Captain Newman's Journal
http://content.wisconsinhistory.org/cdm/ref/collection/wmh/id/829
https://books.google.com/books?id=UDxBU0JfgjMC&pg=PA62&lpg=PA62&dq=fort+ha
milton+september+19+1791&source=bl&ots=4plbLozxT4&sig=rjZuCbWNbxhBXE_0IYj_b0
G9Si0&hl=en&sa=X&ved=2ahUKEwjViaX11cbcAhXl3YMKHVZ4DnUQ6AEwBHoECAQQ
AQ#v=onepage&q=fort%20hamilton%20september%2019%201791&f=false
http://www.brooklineconnection.com/history/Facts/FortPitt.html

September 07, 1791 - Newman's Company Arrives Muskingum Island
Captain Newman's Journal
http://content.wisconsinhistory.org/cdm/ref/collection/wmh/id/829

September 07, 1791 - Quartermaster General Samuel Hodgdon Arrives Fort Washington
http://npshistory.com/series/symposia/george_rogers_clark/1983-1984/sec6.htm
http://www.quartermaster.army.mil/bios/previous-qm-
generals/quartermaster_general_bio-hodgdon.html
September 10, 1791 - Construction Begins on Fort Hamilton
https://www.findagrave.com/memorial/43748513/william-darke
http://www.lva.virginia.gov/public/dvb/bio.asp?b=Darke_William
https://sites.google.com/a/lanepl.org/columns-by-jim-blount/home/2015-
articles/plans-for-navigable-great-miami-river-preceded-arrival-of-first-soldiers-at-fort-
hamilton-in-1791
https://books.google.com/books?id=UDxBU0JfgjMC&pg=PA62&lpg=PA62&dq=fort+ha
milton+september+19+1791&source=bl&ots=4plbLozxT4&sig=rjZuCbWNbxhBXE_0IYj_b0
G9Si0&hl=en&sa=X&ved=2ahUKEwjViaX11cbcAhXl3YMKHVZ4DnUQ6AEwBHoECAQQ
AQ#v=onepage&q=fort%20hamilton%20september%2019%201791&f=false
https://www.ohiohistory.org/learn/collections/archaeology/archaeology-
blog/2014/may-2014/fort-jefferson-17911796

September 11, 1791 - Newman's Company Arrives Fort Washington
Captain Newman's Journal
http://content.wisconsinhistory.org/cdm/ref/collection/wmh/id/829

September 15, 1791 - Newman's Company Departs for Fort Hamilton
Captain Newman's Journal
http://content.wisconsinhistory.org/cdm/ref/collection/wmh/id/829

September 17, 1791 - St. Clair's Army Departs Ludlow Station
http://www.ohiohistorycentral.org/w/St._Clair%27s_Defeat
https://en.wikipedia.org/wiki/St._Clair%27s_Defeat
https://www.historicalmarkerproject.com/markers/HM1FY4_ludlows-
station_Cincinnati-OH.html
https://sites.google.com/a/lanepl.org/columns-by-jim-blount/2016-articles/army-s-ill-
fated-march-from-fort-hamilton-excellent-case-study-of-how-not-to-conduct-military-
campaign
https://www.ohiohistory.org/learn/collections/archaeology/archaeology-
blog/2014/may-2014/fort-jefferson-17911796

September 17, 1791 - Newman's Company Arrives Fort Hamilton
Captain Newman's Journal
http://content.wisconsinhistory.org/cdm/ref/collection/wmh/id/829

September 19, 1791 - Newman's Men Kill Rattlesnakes in Camp
Captain Newman's Journal
http://content.wisconsinhistory.org/cdm/ref/collection/wmh/id/829

September 21, 1791 - St. Clair Receives Information from Vincennes
https://books.google.com/books?id=UDxBU0JfgjMC&pg=PA62&lpg=PA62&dq=fort+ha
milton+september+19+1791&source=bl&ots=4plbLozxT4&sig=rjZuCbWNbxhBXE_0IYj_b0
G9Si0&hl=en&sa=X&ved=2ahUKEwjViaX11cbcAhXl3YMKHVZ4DnUQ6AEwBHoECAQQ
AQ#v=onepage&q=fort%20hamilton%20september%2019%201791&f=false
https://sites.google.com/a/lanepl.org/columns-by-jim-blount/2016-articles/army-s-ill-
fated-march-from-fort-hamilton-excellent-case-study-of-how-not-to-conduct-military-
campaign

September 26, 1791 - Four of Newman's Men Desert
September 28, 1791 - Two of Newman's Men Disappear
September 29, 1791 - Brothers Depew Turn Up
Captain Newman's Journal
http://content.wisconsinhistory.org/cdm/ref/collection/wmh/id/829

September 30, 1791 - Captain Newman's Men Help Finish Fort Hamilton
https://www.nps.gov/tps/how-to-preserve/currents/earthworks/glossary.htm
http://www.butlercountyohio.org/monument/index.cfm?page=fthamilton
http://npshistory.com/series/symposia/george_rogers_clark/1983-1984/sec5.htm
https://www.nps.gov/tps/how-to-preserve/currents/earthworks/glossary.htm
https://en.wikipedia.org/wiki/Palisade

October 01, 1791 - Warriors Kill Men and Steal Horses Near Fort
http://npshistory.com/series/symposia/george_rogers_clark/1983-1984/sec5.htm
Captain Newman's Journal
http://content.wisconsinhistory.org/cdm/ref/collection/wmh/id/829

October 04, 1791 - St. Clair's Army Departs Fort Hamilton
http://content.wisconsinhistory.org/cdm/ref/collection/wmh/id/829
https://sites.google.com/a/lanepl.org/columns-by-jim-blount/2016-articles/army-s-ill-
fated-march-from-fort-hamilton-excellent-case-study-of-how-not-to-conduct-military-
campaign
Captain Newman's Journal
http://content.wisconsinhistory.org/cdm/ref/collection/wmh/id/829

October 13, 1791 - Captain Newman's Company Arrives at Site of Fort Jefferson
https://www.ohiohistory.org/learn/collections/archaeology/archaeology-blog/2014/may-2014/fort-jefferson-17911796
Captain Newman's Journal
http://content.wisconsinhistory.org/cdm/ref/collection/wmh/id/829

October 13, 1791 - Construction Begins on Fort Jefferson
https://www.ohiohistory.org/learn/collections/archaeology/archaeology-blog/2014/may-2014/fort-jefferson-17911796
https://en.wikipedia.org/wiki/Fort_Jefferson_(Ohio)
https://www.ohiohistory.org/visit/museum-and-site-locator/fort-jefferson-park
http://touringohio.com/history/fort-jefferson.html
The Soldiers of America's First Army, 1791
By Richard M. Lytle
https://books.google.com/books?id=UDxBU0JfgjMC&pg=PA80&lpg=PA80&dq=soldiers+hanged+fort+jefferson+1791&source=bl&ots=4pliDqAuQ6&sig=ssShX1fQpINlPhQbJU2psZ9SlvU&hl=en&sa=X&ved=2ahUKEwitvtHc2_vdAhVL5YMKHSwLBDQQ6AEwBXoECAYQAQ#v=onepage&q=soldiers%20hanged%20fort%20jefferson%201791&f=false

October 18, 1791 - Six Men Desert - 60 Horse Convoy of Supplies Arrive
Captain Newman's Journal
http://content.wisconsinhistory.org/cdm/ref/collection/wmh/id/829
https://sites.google.com/a/lanepl.org/columns-by-jim-blount/2016-articles/army-s-ill-fated-march-from-fort-hamilton-excellent-case-study-of-how-not-to-conduct-military-campaign
The Soldiers of America's First Army, 1791
By Richard M. Lytle
https://books.google.com/books?id=UDxBU0JfgjMC&pg=PA80&lpg=PA80&dq=soldiers+hanged+fort+jefferson+1791&source=bl&ots=4pliDqAuQ6&sig=ssShX1fQpINlPhQbJU2psZ9SlvU&hl=en&sa=X&ved=2ahUKEwitvtHc2_vdAhVL5YMKHSwLBDQQ6AEwBXoECAYQAQ#v=onepage&q=soldiers%20hanged%20fort%20jefferson%201791&f=false

October 19, 1791 - General St. Clair Holds Staff Meeting
The Soldiers of America's First Army, 1791
By Richard M. Lytle
https://books.google.com/books?id=UDxBU0JfgjMC&pg=PA80&lpg=PA80&dq=soldiers+hanged+fort+jefferson+1791&source=bl&ots=4pliDqAuQ6&sig=ssShX1fQpINlPhQbJU2psZ9SlvU&hl=en&sa=X&ved=2ahUKEwitvtHc2_vdAhVL5YMKHSwLBDQQ6AEwBXoECAYQAQ#v=onepage&q=soldiers%20hanged%20fort%20jefferson%201791&f=false

October 20, 1791- Enlistments Begin to Run Out
The Soldiers of America's First Army, 1791
By Richard M. Lytle
https://books.google.com/books?id=UDxBU0JfgjMC&pg=PA80&lpg=PA80&dq=soldiers+hanged+fort+jefferson+1791&source=bl&ots=4pliDqAuQ6&sig=ssShX1fQpINlPhQbJU2psZ9SlvU&hl=en&sa=X&ved=2ahUKEwitvtHc2_vdAhVL5YMKHSwLBDQQ6AEwBXoECAYQAQ#v=onepage&q=soldiers%20hanged%20fort%20jefferson%201791&f=false

October 21, 1791 - Twenty Men Desert
Captain Newman's Journal
http://content.wisconsinhistory.org/cdm/ref/collection/wmh/id/829
The Soldiers of America's First Army, 1791
By Richard M. Lytle
https://books.google.com/books?id=UDxBU0JfgjMC&pg=PA80&lpg=PA80&dq=soldiers
+hanged+fort+jefferson+1791&source=bl&ots=4pliDqAuQ6&sig=ssShX1fQpINlPhQbJU2p
sZ9SlvU&hl=en&sa=X&ved=2ahUKEwitvtHc2_vdAhVL5YMKHSwLBDQQ6AEwBXoEC
AYQAQ#v=onepage&q=soldiers%20hanged%20fort%20jefferson%201791&f=false

October 22, 1791 - Deserters Captured
The Soldiers of America's First Army, 1791
By Richard M. Lytle
https://books.google.com/books?id=UDxBU0JfgjMC&pg=PA80&lpg=PA80&dq=soldiers
+hanged+fort+jefferson+1791&source=bl&ots=4pliDqAuQ6&sig=ssShX1fQpINlPhQbJU2p
sZ9SlvU&hl=en&sa=X&ved=2ahUKEwitvtHc2_vdAhVL5YMKHSwLBDQQ6AEwBXoEC
AYQAQ#v=onepage&q=soldiers%20hanged%20fort%20jefferson%201791&f=false
Captain Newman's Journal
http://content.wisconsinhistory.org/cdm/ref/collection/wmh/id/829

October 22, 1791 - Deserters Captured
The Soldiers of America's First Army, 1791
By Richard M. Lytle
https://books.google.com/books?id=UDxBU0JfgjMC&pg=PA80&lpg=PA80&dq=soldiers
+hanged+fort+jefferson+1791&source=bl&ots=4pliDqAuQ6&sig=ssShX1fQpINlPhQbJU2p
sZ9SlvU&hl=en&sa=X&ved=2ahUKEwitvtHc2_vdAhVL5YMKHSwLBDQQ6AEwBXoEC
AYQAQ#v=onepage&q=soldiers%20hanged%20fort%20jefferson%201791&f=false
Captain Newman's Journal
http://content.wisconsinhistory.org/cdm/ref/collection/wmh/id/829

October 24, 1791 - St. Clair's Army Departs
https://www.ohiohistory.org/learn/collections/archaeology/archaeology-
blog/2014/may-2014/fort-jefferson-17911796
https://en.wikipedia.org/wiki/Fort_Jefferson_(Ohio)
https://www.ohiohistory.org/visit/museum-and-site-locator/fort-jefferson-park
http://touringohio.com/history/fort-jefferson.html
The Soldiers of America's First Army, 1791
By Richard M. Lytle
https://books.google.com/books?id=UDxBU0JfgjMC&pg=PA80&lpg=PA80&dq=soldiers
+hanged+fort+jefferson+1791&source=bl&ots=4pliDqAuQ6&sig=ssShX1fQpINlPhQbJU2p
sZ9SlvU&hl=en&sa=X&ved=2ahUKEwitvtHc2_vdAhVL5YMKHSwLBDQQ6AEwBXoEC
AYQAQ#v=onepage&q=soldiers%20hanged%20fort%20jefferson%201791&f=false

October 27, 1791 - Thirteen Men Demand Discharge
https://sites.google.com/a/lanepl.org/columns-by-jim-blount/2016-articles/army-s-ill-
fated-march-from-fort-hamilton-excellent-case-study-of-how-not-to-conduct-military-
campaign
The Soldiers of America's First Army, 1791
By Richard M. Lytle
https://books.google.com/books?id=UDxBU0JfgjMC&pg=PA80&lpg=PA80&dq=soldiers
+hanged+fort+jefferson+1791&source=bl&ots=4pliDqAuQ6&sig=ssShX1fQpINlPhQbJU2p
sZ9SlvU&hl=en&sa=X&ved=2ahUKEwitvtHc2_vdAhVL5YMKHSwLBDQQ6AEwBXoEC
AYQAQ#v=onepage&q=soldiers%20hanged%20fort%20jefferson%201791&f=false

October 29, 1791 - St. Clair Deploys First Scouts
https://sites.google.com/a/lanepl.org/columns-by-jim-blount/2016-articles/army-s-ill-fated-march-from-fort-hamilton-excellent-case-study-of-how-not-to-conduct-military-campaign
https://en.wikipedia.org/wiki/Chickasaw
https://www.chickasaw.net/Our-Nation/History.aspx

October 31, 1791 - Sixty Men Desert
https://sites.google.com/a/lanepl.org/columns-by-jim-blount/2016-articles/army-s-ill-fated-march-from-fort-hamilton-excellent-case-study-of-how-not-to-conduct-military-campaign
https://www.army.mil/article/65594/st_clairs_campaign_of_1791_a_defeat_in_the_wilderness_that_helped_forge_todays_us_army
http://npshistory.com/series/symposia/george_rogers_clark/1983-1984/sec6.htm
The Soldiers of America's First Army, 1791
Richard M. Lytle
https://books.google.com/books?id=UDxBU0JfgjMC&pg=PA115&lpg=PA115&dq=st+Clair+forces+return+fort+washington+november+1791&source=bl&ots=4pm9KlxvU7&sig=5NmwpEw99HCXhzxlcO3NGjCCu08&hl=en&sa=X&ved=2ahUKEwiworrm06veAhUBpYMKHTHuCR8Q6AEwCHoECAYQAQ#v=onepage&q=st%20Clair%20forces%20return%20fort%20washington%20november%201791&f=false

November 4, 1791 - St. Clair's Defeat or Battle of the Wabash
https://armyhistory.org/the-battle-of-the-wabash-the-forgotten-disaster-of-the-indian-wars/
https://en.wikipedia.org/wiki/St._Clair%27s_Defeat
The Soldiers of America's First Army, 1791
By Richard M. Lytle
https://books.google.com/books?id=UDxBU0JfgjMC&pg=PA115&lpg=PA115&dq=st+Clair+forces+return+fort+washington+november+1791&source=bl&ots=4pm9KlxvU7&sig=5NmwpEw99HCXhzxlcO3NGjCCu08&hl=en&sa=X&ved=2ahUKEwiworrm06veAhUBpYMKHTHuCR8Q6AEwCHoECAYQAQ#v=onepage&q=st%20Clair%20forces%20return%20fort%20washington%20november%201791&f=false

About the Author

Paul considers himself a bit of an Indiana hound, in that he likes to sniff out the interesting places and history of Indiana and use his books to tell people about them.

Join Paul on Facebook
https://www.facebook.com/Mossy-Feet-Books-474924602565571/
Twitter
https://twitter.com/MossyFeetBooks
mossyfeetbooks@gmail.com

Mossy Feet Books Catalog

To Get Your Free Copy of the Mossy Feet Books Catalogue, Click This Link.

http://mossyfeetbooks.blogspot.com/

Gardening Books

Fantasy Books

Humor

Science Fiction

Semi – Autobiographical Books

Travel Books

Sample Chapter

A Timeline of Indiana History - 1792 - 1801

January 24, 1792 - Wilkinson Departs for Fort Jefferson

Lieutenant Colonel James Wilkinson had assumed temporary command of the Second Regiment in December 1791 stationed at Fort Washington when General Arthur St. Clair departed for Philadelphia. St Clair had departed to report on the disaster that had befallen his army on November 4, 1791.

Bury the Dead and Attack

Wilkinson's mission had three main objectives:

Provide supplies for the desperate troops stationed at Fort Jefferson

Visit the battlefield and bury the dead

Recover cannon and other valuable supplies left on the battlefield

Attack an Indian village fifteen miles from the battlefield, which was on the banks of a tributary of the Wabash River.

Earlier in the month, Wilkinson had issued a call for 150 volunteers for the mission. About the required number of men had responded, Wilkinson readied his force, which would be composed of the 150 volunteers and about 50 regular troops. Future Indiana Territorial Governor William Henry Harrison served as an ensign during this mission.

Departure

Wilkinson departed Fort Washington during a cold snap that had frozen the Ohio River. Snow two feet deep covered the ground and progress was slow, as the cavalry had to clear the way with their horses for the infantry that followed.

Major David Ziegler had led an earlier relief mission in December 1791. He encountered 116 starving survivors. To survive these men ate horsemeat and hides. Ziegler left supplies for them and returned to Fort Washington.

Mossy Feet Books
www.mossyfeetbooks.com